AF428708

Praise for Becoming Spartan

"You'll see a thousand 'no-limits' business books. This one is different. It's the unglamorous work of turning chaos into systems, written by someone who actually did it. If you've ever had to build something real with nothing but constraints and your brain, you'll recognize yourself on every page."

— Jason Newman, SVP, Marketing Strategy, Audacy

"Brian captures something incredibly important in Becoming Spartan, friction isn't something to avoid, it's something to leverage. Whether it's three people in the woods with two bikes or a high-stakes sales pursuit that could go sideways at any moment, success comes down to adaptability, trust, and execution when conditions are far from perfect. The book is filled with lessons that apply just as much in the woods as they do in the boardroom."

John Boccuzzi, Jr. - President ISG Research

BECOMING

SPARTAN

Leveraging Friction to Forge, Scale, and Outlast

Brian Duncanson

BECOMING SPARTAN

Leveraging Friction to Forge, Scale, and Outlast

PUBLISHING DATA
First Edition: June 2026
Published in the United States of America **Vero Beach, Florida**
ISBN: [979-8-9958698-0-1] (Hardcover)
ISBN: [979-8-9958698-2-5] (Paperback)
ISBN: [979-8-9958698-1-8] (E-book)
Library of Congress Control Number: 2026911040
Cover Design: Eric Cavoli
Interior Design & Layout: The Navigator's Studio
Printed in the United States of America 10 9 8 7 6 5 4 3 2 1

For bulk orders, speaking engagements, or DEKA affiliation inquiries:
Visit: https://www.linkedin.com/in/brian-duncanson-6825971a/ or contact: brian_duncanson@yahoo.com.

FOR

My parents who taught me.
My wife and best friend.
My children.

BECOMING SPARTAN: NAVIGATOR'S MAP

FOREWORD

The View from the Vortex

By Joe De Sena, Founder & CEO, Spartan

The world is soft.

We've optimized every ounce of discomfort out of our lives. We have climate-controlled houses, food delivered by an app, and chairs ergonomically designed to help us rot faster. We are literally dying of comfort.

When I met Brian, I was looking for people who were crazy enough to reject that reality. I was looking for the fire-breathers, the ones who didn't want a participation trophy, but a scar to prove they had survived.

In the early days of Spartan, it was pure chaos. We didn't have a corporate handbook. We had a farm in Vermont, some heavy logs, and a shared belief: if you push a human being to the point of total physical and mental exhaustion, they don't break. They finally wake up.

But a vision without execution is just a hallucination.

I'm the guy who wants to launch a thousand races tomorrow. I want to put a barbed-wire crawl on every street corner in America. But you can't build a global sport on adrenaline and spite alone. You need a navigator. You need someone who can look at the map of a mission and engineer a route to the finish line.

That was Brian.

I wanted to burn the boats; Brian figured out how to build a fleet out of the ashes.

We had a lot of productive friction over the years. We argued, we pushed, and we ground the gears until we forged an operating system that could handle the weight of millions of racers. This book is the history of that grind. It's the raw, gasoline-soaked reality of how we built this empire when everyone else said we were nuts.

But this isn't just a history book. It is a manual.

Read this book if you want to understand how a few guys with a vision built a global movement. But more importantly, read it to understand that the friction in your life isn't your enemy. It is your ultimate advantage.

If you aren't struggling, you aren't growing.

Get off the couch. Sign up for an event. Bring a friend.

AROO!

INTRODUCTION: THE SPARTAN PARADOX

I want to be clear about one thing: Spartan did not succeed because Joe and I were always in agreement. It succeeded because we were almost always in a state of *meaningful friction.*

In mechanics, you need two gears grinding against each other to create movement. If the gears are too soft, they slip; if they are too hard, they shatter. Joe was the centrifugal force, a fire-breather who wanted to annex every mountain on Earth by yesterday. I was the navigator, the one with the maps, the permits, and the technical problem-solving who had to ensure we didn't fly the plane into a cliff.

That friction wasn't a bug; it was a feature. Without Joe's audacity, Spartan would have stayed a local New England race series. Without my systems and operational piracy, Joe's vision might have burned out in a spectacular, unrecorded fireball. We were the Spartan paradox: a partnership built on the productive tension between visionary and integrator.

This book began as a record for the Spartan team to understand our fountainhead energy, but it evolved into a manual for business diamonds forged under pressure. The lessons we learned, often through failure, exhaustion, and near catastrophe, are the only ones that actually matter when the world gets hard.

THE ARCHITECTURE OF BECOMING SPARTAN

To help you navigate this manual, the journey is broken into four distinct phases of Becoming Spartan:

Part I: The Forge (The Ancestry of Grit) traces the lead-up to Spartan and explores the adventure racing heritage that established our baseline for what is humanly possible.

Part II: The Spark (Bootstrapping the Revolution) tells the story of the first year, when Spartan went from a paper-napkin idea to a struggling, high-velocity scramble to keep pace with a movement that was scaling faster than our infrastructure.

Part III: The Superpower (Hyper-Growth Tactics) shows how we executed global dominance by building the global standard, engineering the *trifecta machine*, and weathering the success friction of the hyper-growth era.

Part IV: The Legacy (Unbreakable) follows the pivot to a global institution, the fight to survive the 2020 pandemic through decentralized innovation, and the push to lead the sport to its final peak: the Olympic Games.

THE NAVIGATOR'S LOGIC

While the chapters provide the visceral history and the business theory, each of the four parts concludes with a dedicated "Navigator's Logic." This section is designed to pull you out of our specific story and into your own. It includes the following:

- **Market Mirrors**: Case studies showing how industry leaders like Patagonia, CrossFit, Garmin, and the UFC leverage these same principles to maintain their competitive edge.

- **Monday Morning Protocols**: Tangible, tactical exercises for you to execute within your own context immediately. This is where the theory meets the pavement.

THE FOUR TRIBES

This book is a bridge between four worlds:

To the internal Spartan team: I wrote this so you don't lose the soul in the spreadsheets. We didn't buy this brand; we built it in 2:00 a.m. rainstorms and border-crossing standoffs. My background in adventure racing taught me that you don't always need a perfect plan or a full budget to succeed; you just need to be more resilient than the problem in front of you. When you are staring at a missing 34 percent in your resources, remember: that is where we find our best ideas. Knowing where we came from is the only way to protect where we are going.

To the Spartan faithful: You are the reason we refused to let the gears stop grinding. I have read your stories of transformation. How a single race became the catalyst for a total life reboot. You have seen the course from the starting line. Now, it is time to see the Smoldering Man and the logistics of the chaos from the inside. This is proof that the leaders of this movement were just as unbreakable (and occasionally just as broken) as you.

To the business leaders and the boardroom executives: Comfort is a slow-acting poison. *Becoming Spartan* is a tactical manual for a volatile economy. Whether you lead a Fortune 500 division or a garage startup, use these dirt-stained protocols, like Two-Bike Math and contextual innovation, to out-flank your competition.

To every individual facing an obstacle: This isn't a self-help book, but I have learned that the grit required to build a company is identical to the grit required for personal survival. Whether you are staring down a one-hundred-mile race, a ruthless competitor, or a life-threatening diagnosis in a sterile hospital room, the physics of resilience do not change.

This book is proof that when you are stripped of your gear, your engine is all that remains. We are biologically starving for friction. We need resistance to find out what we are made of. This is the story of how we weaponized that hunger to build a global superpower.

Keep moving forward. Use the friction to light the fire.

AROO!

PREFACE

For the first time in my life, I think I may die tonight.

I have paddled down Class IV rapids, jumped backwards off sheer cliffs attached only to a climbing rope, and been lost in the backwoods of Maine in the middle of the night, but never felt my life was in true danger until now. Curled in a ball, staring at the inside rails of my ICU hospital bed filled with indicator lights, I think: this is how a lot of people die. In this position, in this room, maybe even in this bed — alone. The big procedure is tomorrow and it is clear to me now that I won't be able to sleep.

The cocktail of drugs the doctors gave me has hit me like never before. This is my fourth round of high-dose chemotherapy and the doctors have added a drug commonly known as "The Rabbit" on top of it. All of it has brought me to zero. The expected pain is so great they hooked up a morphine drip and gave me a controller that would release more drugs if I needed them. It seems crazy to have that much autonomy over substances I have never taken before, nor have any idea how they will affect me. I make up my mind that I will not press the button. I've been in pain many times before.

At 3:00am the alarm went off for the third time tonight, sending the nurse rushing into my room ready to jump into action. The monitor indicated that my heart rate was critically low. Years of endurance training gave me a naturally low resting heart rate, and combined with the medicine swirling through my body, it had pushed me below thirty beats per minute. I came out of the fog long enough to say I was fine. But I knew I wasn't fine.

I just need to make it through the night. I have been here before — not in this room, not in this bed — but in this specific darkness. Racing for multiple days without sleep, dehydrated, mentally spent, you learn where your true limits lie. You learn that the night lies to you. It tells you it won't end. It tells you to quit. We had a rule in adventure racing: no one quits during the night. The sunrise always changes your outlook.

I just need to survive until morning.

This is what many years of friction was actually preparing me for. Here is how it started.

PROLOGUE: The Gasoline-Soaked Arrow

Catamount Outdoor Center, Williston, VT | May 22, 2010 0900 Hours | Ignition Failure

The archer dipped the tip of his arrow into a bucket of fuel, lit the flame, and drew back his bow.

His target was a twelve-foot straw man, doused in gasoline, standing thirty yards away like a sacrificial totem. Behind him, a crowd of five hundred onlookers held their breath. In the starting corral, the first one hundred athletes in history stood shoulder to shoulder, eyes locked on the flame. They were about to embark on something called a "Spartan Race," though none of them, not even the people running the event, quite knew what that meant yet.

I looked at the archer and gave the nod. He let the arrow fly. It arched through the morning light, a streak of orange against the green pines, and thudded dead center into the chest of the straw man.

And then . . . nothing.

The flame on the arrow flickered and died the moment it hit the straw. No explosion. No wall of fire. Just a dull thud and a wisp of gray smoke.

The silence was deafening. The crowd looked at me. I looked at the "Smoldering Man."

I blew the air horn and yelled, "GO!"

The first heat of athletes didn't care about the pyrotechnics. They charged into the unknown, disappearing into the Vermont woods to find out what "Spartan" really meant.

While they ran, the real startup work began. My teammate Richard didn't have time for cinematic arrows. He grabbed a container of gasoline and began dousing the straw man by hand. As I watched him, all I could think about was the straw man and Richard going up in flames together in a catastrophic fireball. He worked at it for minutes, ignoring his personal safety, until finally—whoosh—the straw man roared to life.

By the time the second heat of athletes arrived, the fire was magnificent. They saw the burning legend. They didn't see Richard and the gas can.

This was the moment of birth for Spartan.

I'd love to tell you this moment was the result of years of meticulous corporate planning and professional execution. I'd love to tell you we were a polished machine.

But the truth is, the straw man didn't light, the course was too short, we ran out of parking space and had to stuff cars down the road, and the waivers were late arriving, causing a massive backup of frustrated customers at check-in. The truth is, we were making it up as we went. Five months earlier, this brand didn't even have a name. It was just an idea on a paper napkin.

PART I: THE FORGE (1999–2009)

The Ancestry of Grit and the DNA of Perpetual Adaptation

The core DNA of a brand is not written in a mission statement; it is forged in its most extreme early tests. Before Spartan was a race, it was an endurance laboratory, a multi-day crucible where sleep was a luxury and navigation was a weapon. In "The Forge," you learn that business isn't a sprint between milestones; it's a nonstop, hundred-mile navigation through shifting terrain. If your team cannot adapt to a 3:00 a.m. crisis with minimum resources, they will never survive the complexities of a global market.

1999–2009 | Various Locations

The Soul of the Brand

To truly understand the lineage of Spartan, we must go back to the landscape before the spark that started it all.

We have to go back to a time when a chaotic, unregulated sport called *adventure racing* was clawing its way from the fringe into the mainstream. Races varied in length from four hours to seven days. You raced with a team of three or four people across various terrain, finding your way with maps and a compass. All non-motorized forms of travel were allowed: trekking; mountain biking; paddling in lakes, rivers, or the ocean; mountain climbing and rappelling; glacial traverse with ice axes and crampons; even roller blading in urban settings. It was a discipline that demanded everything and promised nothing, and it captured the obsession of two men on a collision course: myself and Joe De Sena.

This sport did more than just bring us together. It formed the soul of the brand. The friction, the grit, and the refusal to quit, it was all forged here, in the deep woods and long nights, years before the name Spartan ever existed.

You are about to enter a world where the laws of the office don't apply, resources are nonexistent, and the only currency that matters is the ability to solve a problem when you are physically and mentally bankrupt.

Welcome to the Forge.

CHAPTER 1: THE BLACK HOLE FILTER

Building a World-Class Team by Saying No

Building a world-class team or strong customer base starts with who you say no to. This is the story of how a construction pit and a software interview taught me to filter for resilience.

THE STARTING CANNON

September 1999 | Farmington, Connecticut | Hi-Tec Adventure Race

The cannon blast didn't just signal the start of a race; it shattered my assumptions about what a team was capable of. The event was massive, nine hundred of us, a sea of spandex, hydration packs, and unearned confidence, charged forward into the woods. My three-person team was staring down the course, which included miles of trail running, kayaking, and mountain biking, plus unknown obstacles hidden along the way.

At the starting line, everyone looked strong. Everyone looked ready. But races like this have a way of stripping away appearances quickly. The crowd surged forward, slowly at first, then faster and faster. We were now in a full sprint past Winding Trails Lake, which we would paddle in later, and then turned abruptly onto a wooded dirt trail. Once the trail narrowed into a single-track path and the humidity began to take its toll, the truth started to surface. The breathing changed. The pace settled. The effort became real. I had talked two friends into joining me for the race. They were fit, competitive types who liked pushing themselves. But as the miles unfolded, something subtle began to reveal itself. They were there to finish. I was there to be on the podium. That difference didn't show up at the starting line. It showed up when the terrain got ugly.

THE SAND DUNE TEST

Two miles into the run, the trail opened into a massive construction pit. Looming in front of us was a ten-story sand dune. While the lead teams were already cresting the top and disappearing out of sight, the rest of us attacked the slope.

The sand swallowed our feet instantly. Every step slid backward. Within seconds my shoes were full of grit that would grind against my skin for the next five hours. A steep hill is one kind of friction. It challenges you. It forces you to get stronger to reach the top. Sand is different. Sand is parasitic friction. It doesn't build muscle. It drains momentum. It erodes your will.

As the race wore on, I realized something uncomfortable. I was dragging an anchor. My friends were good athletes, but every time the terrain became more demanding, the gap between our expectations widened. We were three capable individuals, but we were not one unit. Meanwhile, the professional teams in their matching logoed race kits moved like a single organism. They didn't negotiate pace. They didn't debate strategy. They simply executed. We finished in over five hours. The professionals did it in half that time. Standing at the finish line, exhausted and frustrated with myself, I realized my selection process had been completely wrong.

TRADING CONVENIENCE FOR GRIT

I had built my team based on convenience and friendship instead of alignment with the mission. I had invited people who wanted to run a race. The sport required people who could survive a catastrophe. Those are not the same thing. The decision I made afterward felt cold at the time, but it was necessary. If I wanted to compete seriously, I needed to change how I built the team. I stopped looking for friends who wanted to participate and started looking for partners who understood suffering. That shift led me to Dave Giampietro, an ex-teammate of mine from Northeastern University's swimming team, and Steve Vadas, a six-foot-four workhorse colleague of mine. Dave became the stabilizer. He understood the long game of endurance, the quiet discipline required to push through hours of discomfort without complaint. Steve was the spark. He had strength, but more importantly, he had the kind of attitude that held firm when things got difficult. With Dave and Steve, something changed immediately. The parasitic friction disappeared. We didn't have to negotiate pace. We didn't argue over gear or energy or commitment. Because we had filtered for alignment before the race began, we could spend our energy fighting the terrain instead of fighting each other. We weren't just faster. We were harder to break. That team eventually took us to the podiums I had been chasing, and it taught me something I would carry into every organization I ever built:

A team's strength is not in the sum of its parts, but in the quality of the filter that lets those parts in.

THE WHITEBOARD GAUNTLET

Years earlier, I ran into the business version of that same lesson. I was interviewing at Bristol Technology, a start-up software company in Connecticut. My interview started not with a one-on-one in Human Resources, but in the lunchroom in front of the entire thirty-person company. I was asked to introduce myself and then answer questions from any one of the employees. They were applying their culture filter to see if I was going to fit in.

The company was loaded with high-IQ engineers solving difficult problems. Even though I was interviewing for a sales position, they wanted the same filter applied to everyone. After surviving a second session of technical interviews, I walked into the final session. I expected a friendly conversation about moving from California to Connecticut and what life was like inside the company. Instead, they handed me a marker and pointed at a whiteboard. For the next hour, two people from the Marketing Department fired bizarre logic puzzles and technical scenarios at me while I worked through them in real time. No introductions. No warm-up. Just pressure.

At first it felt aggressive. Then I realized what they were doing. They weren't evaluating my résumé. They were evaluating how I behaved under strain. A résumé is marketing. Pressure is data. Under pressure, some people complain about the environment. Others keep the marker in their hand and keep working. That hour taught me something I would apply over and over again in building teams. Competence matters, but resilience matters more. I passed the interview and was hired as a sales manager.

After joining the company, I became part of the filtering process as new candidates walked through the door. I learned that anyone in the lunch room could simply email "Ding!" to the CEO, and your fate was sealed. It was brutal, but once a person was hired, they assimilated quickly because they were cut from the same cloth.

THE NAVIGATOR'S LOGIC

Looking back, the race in Farmington and the whiteboard at Bristol were teaching the same lesson. The quality of any team is determined long before the work begins. It is determined by the filter. If the filter is weak, friction shows up everywhere. Energy is wasted negotiating expectations, solving preventable conflicts, and dragging misaligned people through difficult terrain. If the filter is strong, the friction becomes productive. The team moves as a unit. Energy goes toward solving real problems instead of internal ones. A filter that catches nothing is not a filter. It is a window. If you are not actively repelling the wrong people, you are slowly accumulating a crowd. If you are constantly slowing down to accommodate someone who does not share your winning state, you are paying a silent tax on your growth. Most leaders think they are hiring for skill when they should be filtering for grit. It is common for managers to think they have a people problem when what they really have is a filter problem.

The same is true for your customers or clients. Many business owners want every single person as a customer. This works if you are selling a commodity. But if you want loyalists who will bring along their friends, you need to apply a similar filter. It might actually be better for your business to say no to some prospects. If the right amount of friction exists for your customers on the way in, they will feel part of the inner circle, and you will cultivate a group of super fans.

THE MARKET MIRROR: CROSSFIT

Once I started noticing this principle, I began seeing it everywhere. The strongest cultures were rarely the most comfortable ones. They were the clearest ones. You could see it clearly in the fitness world. In the early 2000s, most gyms were selling comfort. Climate-controlled buildings. Rows of televisions. Soft towels and smooth machines. CrossFit went in the opposite direction. They moved workouts into garages. They removed the machines. They created environments that were intentionally demanding. To an outsider it looked like bad marketing. But it was actually brilliant filtration. By repelling the casual gym-goer, CrossFit attracted a tribe. The friction of the environment wasn't a flaw. It was the selection filter. What looked harsh from the outside was simply honesty: "This is not for everyone." That clarity built loyalty. The same thing is true in any market. If you are trying to be attractive to everyone, you usually end up standing for nothing. The strongest brands and the strongest teams know who they are for, but they also know who they are not for. That difference matters.

MONDAY MORNING PROTOCOLS

Once you understand the power of selection filters, the question becomes how to apply them.

1. The first filter is internal. Résumés are marketing; actions are data. Before making a final hiring decision, give candidates a stress-test assignment with a tight deadline. One candidate complains about the short notice. Another candidate completes the work and suggests a way to improve the process. The difference between those two reactions tells you more than a résumé ever will.
2. The second filter is external. Many organizations try to appeal to everyone, and the result is that they attract people who have no real commitment to the mission. A stronger approach is to define clearly who the organization is not for. A simple statement on a website or in recruiting material can act as a powerful filter: "If you want a participation trophy, this process will frustrate you." That kind of message repels mercenaries and attracts missionaries.
3. The third filter is energy. Not every customer belongs in the system. Some clients create high profit with very little friction. Others create constant drag while producing minimal value. Over time, those relationships become sand in the gearbox. Segmenting clients into four groups by high/low profit and high/low friction allows leaders to see where their energy is going and where capacity can be reclaimed. Protecting that energy is one of the most important responsibilities of leadership.

Once you have filtered for a team that doesn't just survive the sand in their shoes but uses it to calibrate their grit, you finally have the engine required for real momentum. But even the most powerful engine is wasted if it's stuck in a bottleneck. To win, your team must stop waiting for a clear path and start identifying the gaps, the unconventional routes the rest of the market is too crowded to see. That's where the next lesson begins.

CHAPTER 2: OPERATIONAL PIRACY

Acting in the Silence of the Rules to Out-Maneuver the Competition

 The most successful organizations don't wait for permission; they act in the silence of the rules and force the world to adapt to them. This chapter is about identifying the *stealth vectors* that allow you to out-maneuver the competition before they even realize the game has started.

BUSHWHACKING

New River Gorge, West Virginia | May 2001 | The Endorphin Fix, Hour 16

"The road goes that way," my teammate said. His voice was tight with exhaustion, the sound of a man who had been awake and moving for thirty hours and was down to his last reserves of patience.

"I know," I replied, pointing to the race map. Its edges were soft and frayed from sweat and humidity. "I know where the road goes. It winds around the mountain in a series of switchbacks. It's a five-mile detour designed for cars. There's a faster way."

We were sixteen hours into a 48-hour adventure race, standing at a gravel intersection in the West Virginia backcountry. These were the kind of narrow tracks where two cars passing each other required both to slide into a ditch. The sun was dipping toward the horizon, casting long shadows. The next checkpoint was a rock outcropping where we'd learned to rope climb and rappel earlier that week. I wanted to hit that point before nightfall, mostly because I didn't want to be navigating a cliff side in the dark with a headlamp.

THE DIRECT AZIMUTH

Navigator's Note: In land navigation, an Azimuth is simply your True Heading. While a road is a winding path built by someone else, an azimuth is a straight line drawn from where you are to where you need to be. It is the shortest distance between two points, usually requiring you to leave the comfort of the trail and move directly through the friction of the terrain.

If we followed the road, we would arrive after dark. That was a high-risk move disguised as safety. If we left the road for the forest, we could arrive in the daylight. That was a calculated risk.

"If we shoot an azimuth directly from here to the checkpoint, we save over an hour," I said to my three teammates. I didn't wait for a vote. I lined up the baseplate compass, rotated the bezel to the bearing, and pointed directly into the thick, unbroken woods. "Follow me."

We bushwhacked up a steep grade, scrambled through thorns, and inadvertently cut through someone's backyard before crossing back onto a higher road. That single decision to ignore the intended trail and take a direct route moved us from tenth place to fourth. That mindset of cutting through the noise didn't just apply to physical navigation; it applied to the rulebook itself. I call this *operational piracy*—the art of finding the invisible path that the organizers didn't see.

THE KITE HACK

Columbia River, Hood River, Oregon | July 2001 | Gorge Games 24-Hour Adventure Race

The physics didn't make sense. A three-person kayak was tearing down the center of the Columbia River, throwing up a wake like a motorboat. But if you looked closely, the paddles were resting on the athletes' laps. No one was rowing.

At the front of the boat, Robyn Benincasa, a world-class adventure racer was leaning back with all her might, fighting the tension of two lines. High above the water, a massive traction kite, the kind usually attached to a kite boarder, was filled with the gorge's legendary wind. Robyn had simply looked at the environment and pirated a solution. While Dave, Steve, and I were paddling against the waves and wind like the other teams, her team was drinking water and surfing.

The kite became a problem, though, as Robyn's kayak approached a bridge. They had to reel it in quickly to avoid getting hung up on the span. The race organizers were furious. They had written a thick rulebook, but they had made a fatal assumption: they assumed everyone would paddle. They checked the book. Did it say No kites? No. Did it say human power only? No. It just said, "Travel by kayak." Robyn traveled by kayak; she just let the wind do the work.

FINDING THE SILENCE IN THE RULES

Most teams read the rules to find out what they have to do. The pirate reads the rules to find out what they didn't say.

I saw this play out at a Balance Bar 24-Hour Adventure Race in New Jersey, where a rule stated: "Bike tires cannot touch the ground during the navigation leg." The race director's intent was to force teams to carry their heavy bikes for miles through the woods. While every other team, including mine, struggled under the weight over the rocky terrain, the winning team simply flipped their bikes upside down and left them. Technically, the tires weren't touching the ground; the handlebars were. They ran unencumbered to the checkpoint and then backtracked for the bikes, riding the paved road around the mountain rather than carrying their bikes over it.

This isn't just about breaking the rules; it's about identifying the gap between a new innovation and the rules designed for the old world. While your competitors wait for a green light from a regulator or a board of directors, the navigator is already moving down the invisible path.

THE PIRATE PARABLE: KIDNAPPING THE BEAR

I realized the ultimate business application of this logic when I looked at the rivalry between Coca-Cola and Pepsi. For decades, Coke spent billions building the Polar Bear into a global icon of happiness and tradition. The bear was Coke. It was an institutional asset: safe, expensive, and universally recognized.

During a Super Bowl campaign, Pepsi didn't try to invent a better animal. They didn't spend millions trying to make a Pepsi Penguin. They simply kidnapped the Bear. They ran ads showing the iconic Coke Polar Bears cheating on their employer. They showed the bears on vacation, taking off their Coke fur and cracking open a crisp, cold Pepsi. Pepsi realized that Coke had done all the heavy lifting to make the audience love the bears. By showing the bears preferring Pepsi, they used Coke's multi-billion-dollar budget to sell their own product.

This is the essence of operational piracy: You don't always need to build your own icons or infrastructure from scratch. Sometimes, the most efficient route is to identify an existing highway built by your competitor and find the loophole that lets you drive on it for free.

THE NAVIGATOR'S LOGIC

In the corporate world, people seek clarification until every gray area is illuminated. In a high-stakes startup, that is a strategic mistake. If you ask for permission, you give the world a chance to say no. If you act in silence, you achieve social gravity before the competition even realizes the game has started. This comfort with the gray zone, the ability to look at an unregulated landscape and see opportunity instead of chaos, isn't something you learn in a boardroom. It's an instinct forged in environments where the rules haven't been written yet.

Identify the stealth vector by looking for the route the competition is too afraid to take. Whether it's bushwhacking through a forest or using a different legal interpretation of a contract, the most efficient path is rarely the one everyone else is following. Stop asking questions. If you have a tactical advantage and the rules don't explicitly forbid it, execute. Asking for clarification only serves to close the loophole for everyone else. Leverage regulatory arbitrage. There is always latency between a new idea and the regulations designed to control it. Move into that gap. By the time the rules catch up to you, you might already be the market leader.

THE MARKET MIRROR: UBER

Uber realized taxi regulations only applied to taxis. They launched a stealth vector in the gray zone of municipal law. They positioned themselves as a technology platform rather than a transportation company, bypassing the traditional hurdles of medallion systems, where only licensed taxis could legally pick up passengers, until they were too big to be shut down. By the time regulators woke up, Uber had already achieved social gravity. They didn't break the law; they lived in the silence of it.

MONDAY MORNING PROTOCOLS

1. The Habit Audit: Identify one rule your company follows that is actually just a habit, something you do because "that's how it's always been done." Break it this week to test for efficiency.
2. The Silence Protocol: Run one low-cost, high-reward experiment in the gray zone where the rules are unwritten or ambiguous. If it fails, kill it quietly. If it wins, present the data.
3. The Asset Hijack: Identify your competitor's most expensive asset. How can you legally draft off their wake?

In adventure racing, you are only as good as your preparation. You spend months conditioning the body so that when the mind eventually breaks, the machine keeps moving. But that ability to look at a desperate situation and find a hidden advantage isn't learned in a gym; it's formed over a lifetime of exposure to friction.

When a team is handed coordinates and a map, the tension is high. You have to plot the destination with surgical precision. But there is a moment where the ink has to dry. The navigator must fold the map, step into the dark, and lead. Before I was architecting corporate strategy for millions, I was navigating the raw physics of the wild. To understand the Spartan operating system, we have to go back to the original laboratory: the woods, the water, and the high-stakes friction of a 1970s neighborhood.

CHAPTER 3: THE STRESS LABORATORY

Setting a Calibrated Baseline for Resilience

 Resilience is not a personality trait; it is a calibrated baseline. This chapter is about how a decade of meaningful friction in the woods and the water became the DNA of the Spartan operating system.

August 2000 | Sabah, Borneo | Eco-Challenge Adventure Race

GUEST DISPATCH: IAN ADAMSON (10x World Champion Adventure Racer)

In the pre-dawn humidity of the Sabah jungle, the air doesn't just sit on you; it weighs you down. We were five days into the Eco-Challenge, and the plan had long since been incinerated. In adventure racing, the enemy isn't the terrain; it is entropy— the constant, grinding decay of your gear, your body, and your team's chemistry.

I've always looked at a race course as a series of physics problems. But in Borneo, I was dealing with a variable I couldn't solve on a calculator: Robyn Benincasa.

Robyn is a fire-breather. She is pure, unadulterated "Go." But in the final transition going into the water leg, the friction between us was reaching a flashpoint. I was hunched over the maps, my mind deep in the sailing charts and wind patterns of the South China Sea. I wasn't looking for the shortest route; I was looking for the fastest route. There is a massive difference.

Robyn was vibrating. She wanted to be in the boats. Every second we spent on the beach was a second our competitors, the French and the Aussies, were closing the gap. To her, my deliberation looked like hesitation. To me, her urgency looked like a shortcut to disaster.

"Ian, we have to move," she snapped. It wasn't a suggestion.

I didn't look up. "Going fast in the wrong direction isn't moving, Robyn. It's just getting lost with more velocity."

I knew that the other teams could paddle faster than us. If we paddled straight for the finish, they would simply sit on our wake and out-power us. So, I plotted a course that looked like a mistake—a stealth vector. I used my knowledge of local tides and wind drift to plot a non-obvious route into a chain of islands.

I could feel the team's doubt. We were paddling northwest while the finish line was to the northeast. Paddling away from the goal feels like a betrayal of instinct. But six hours later, when we hit the final beach, we hadn't just finished, we had won. We arrived hours ahead of faster teams because we had mastered the map while they had only mastered the muscle.

THE TREE GAME

That ability to calculate while the world is screaming at you is forged in a *stress laboratory*. My first lab didn't involve global championships; it involved a nylon rope and an oak tree in Bullville, New York, in 1978. I was ten years old, playing Manhunt with ten other older boys. If they caught you, you were tied to a tree with rope, and then they would vanish into the woods to hunt your other friends.

One day I was one of the first caught. There were no parents coming. No referee. Panic started to rise, that primal fear of being trapped. But then, a colder instinct took over.

I realized that if I worked at the knots long enough, they would come loose and I could wiggle out. It took twenty minutes of grinding, but I slipped free. I didn't run home crying. I ran back into the woods to find my friend. The game wasn't over. The woods weren't a playground; they were a classroom where the only rule was survival.

THE WILDERNESS MBA

My parents were school teachers, so we used our summers to drive across the country. Camping wasn't a hobby; it was our housing. I grew up with the smell of canvas and wood smoke permanently etched into my memory. We navigated the country with paper road maps, then used trail maps to hike. By the time I reached high school, I had visited most of the National Parks in the US. I slept on the floor of the Grand Canyon, stood on the top of Mt. Washington, and paddled past alligators in Florida rivers. Deep in the woods, there is no customer service. You pack all of your supplies, and you learn that a mistake in reading a map at 2:00 p.m. means you are shivering in the dark at 8:00 p.m. This comfort with the law of consequences, if you don't secure the food, the bears take it, became the foundation of the process that later saved Spartan a dozen times over.

THE CHLORINE BASELINE

In college, that classroom moved to the Northeastern University natatorium. I spent my mornings and afternoons in a sensory deprivation tank, a lane of churned water in the middle of a Boston winter. You could smell the chlorine long before you reached the pool doors; it lived in your pores. While my teammates focused on the clock, I used the black line on the pool floor as a mental workbench. As a computer science and math major, I would mentally draft lines of code or work through calculus proofs while my body was in a state of total hypoxia. I was honing my problem-solving skills while training for D1 competition. This was cognitive stress testing. It taught me how to keep the analytical engine running even when the physical gear was redlined.

At Northeastern, we didn't have separate practice for the women's and men's teams. Due to the co-op program, half of the team was in school and the other half working jobs. The fix was to have one early afternoon session for the school crowd and a late session for the working group. This meant that the men and women practiced together. The women's team was loaded with full scholarship athletes since the school had to even out all of the football scholarships. The men's team only had partial scholarships. Being beaten by the women's team in workouts stripped my ego. It taught me that gender is irrelevant to grit, a lesson that led me to seek out elite women as teammates in adventure racing. This is also where I first met my swimming teammate, Dave Giampietro, who would later become part of my adventure racing journey.

REIGNITION

After college, I moved out to California and started working for Teradyne, a Fortune 500 company that manufactured semiconductor testing equipment, as a software engineer. I left the competitive athletic space behind for a softer life of golf and weekends playing volleyball on the Malibu beach. I took the opportunity to get my MBA from Pepperdine University, which led me to the job at Bristol Technology in 1995 in Connecticut.

It was there that I began to get the competitive fire again and started training for triathlons. It was at a local race that I ran into Dave Giampietro, who happened to live just a few towns away.

Then one day I was flipping through the television stations when I stumbled upon the Eco-Challenge. There I was, watching Ian Adamson and Robyn Bennicasa sprinting through the Borneo jungle. I was hooked instantly. The sport spoke to my competitiveness, my outdoor adventure spirit, and my problem-solving nature. I found the Hi-Tec Racing Series, which had an event in Connecticut, and signed up with my friends. That was the start of a journey that would put me on a path to meet Joe De Sena.

THE TRIPLE WITCH OF SUFFERING

By the mid-2000s, a few hundred miles away, Joe De Sena was conducting his own audit of the human will. On Wall Street, a *triple witching day* is a high-volatility event where three types of contracts expire simultaneously on the third Friday of the final month of each quarter. Joe decided to apply that same pressure to his own biology. In a span of just ten days, he completed three of the most grueling endurance events on the planet: Ironman, the Badwater 135, and the Vermont 100. Most elite athletes train for six months for just one of these. Joe treated them like a Tuesday. He was looking for the system floor, the absolute limit where the body is spent and the mind must take over 100 percent of the load. We were two vectors on a collision course. Joe wanted to find the breaking point; I wanted to map the way through it.

I later learned that Mike Pape, a friend of mine from high school, had become Joe's personal trainer in New York City. He told me, before I knew who Joe was, that he had a client who just wanted Mike to hurt him. Mike would design crazy-hard workouts, and Joe would simply challenge him to make it even harder.

THE NAVIGATOR'S LOGIC

Resilience is not a personality trait; it is a calibrated baseline. If your operational baseline is set in a climate-controlled office, any real friction will shatter your team. In a crisis, you must learn to strip away the emotion. You don't get angry at a math equation; you just solve for the variables. View a market crash or a logistical failure as a set of data points to be navigated. Understand where your team actually breaks. Most people quit at 40 percent of their actual capacity because their comfort baseline is too high.

Master the map, not just the muscle. As Ian Adamson proved in Borneo, high-velocity movement in the wrong direction is just a faster way to fail. The navigator's job is to calculate the vector that allows you to outmaneuver competitors who are relying on raw effort alone.

THE MARKET MIRROR: APPLE

Apple builds operational resilience by assigning a DRI: Directly Responsible Individual, to every important task, decision, or deliverable. That means each action item has one clearly named owner, not a committee and not a vague group. Everyone knows who is responsible for driving it forward, following through, and answering for the outcome. That clarity creates friction, but it is productive friction. It removes the easy escape of shared responsibility and forces real accountability at the individual level. In effect, every person is working in a daily stress laboratory where ownership is visible, expectations are high, and excuses have very little room to survive.

MONDAY MORNING PROTOCOLS

1. The DRI Audit: Assign a single name to your three most important projects this week. If more than one person is in charge, you have a vulnerability.
2. The Drama Log Translation: Take the most emotionally charged problem in your business right now and write it down with adjectives. Then rewrite it using only raw data. Strip the adjectives and the drama until it is just a logic problem.
3. The Voluntary Stress Lab: Schedule one intentional, uncomfortable physical or logistical event for your leadership team this quarter. Remind them what hard actually feels like before the market does it for you.

Having the internal engine to survive the woods is the starting point. But in the early days of any startup, you quickly realize that willpower doesn't pay for plane tickets or equipment. If you want to build a global movement like Spartan on a shoestring budget, you will need to face the reality of extreme scarcity. To win, you have to stop looking at what you lack and start looking at how to optimize what you have. This requires a new kind of arithmetic, a way to make two bikes do the work of three.

CHAPTER 4: TWO-BIKE MATH

Achieving 100 Percent of the Mission with 66 Percent of the Resources

Scarcity is not a budget problem; it is a design challenge. This chapter is about achieving 100 percent of the mission with 66 percent of the resources by mastering the art of shared struggle and rhythmic allocation.

After surviving the six-mile run and three-mile kayak sections
of this race, we hit the transition area exhausted, our shoes
heavy with wet sand and our lungs burning from the humidity.
We expected to grab our mountain bikes and ride out into the
woods for the final leg. Instead, we found a sign posted at the
entrance of the bike corral that changed my business
philosophy forever:

"For the bike leg, teams are permitted only two bicycles."

We were a three-person team. We were already exhausted.
We had twelve miles of technical trail ahead of us. And we
were one bike short. To make matters worse, our female
teammate was barely five feet tall and rode a very small frame.
My friend and I were both six feet. There was no way we could
ride her bike. We were going to have to figure out a solution
that split the running between us.

THE LEAPFROG PROTOCOL

We had to solve a new equation quickly. One person running
next to two riders was incredibly inefficient. The solution was
Two-Bike Math: the art of moving forward when the resources
don't match the requirement. Since doubles, two people riding
one bike, were strictly forbidden for safety, we had to invent a
leapfrog protocol on the fly.

The plan was that I would hammer ahead at a max sprint on
the bike, drop the bike a half mile down the trail, and
immediately start running. My teammate would finish his run,
find the bike in the bushes, mount it, and pedal past the group
to repeat the cycle. The whole team could now move faster. It
was a solid plan.

In the single-track woods, the chaos was absolute. There were bikes strewn across the trails like a metallic graveyard. Because I wasn't 100 percent sure what my teammate's bike looked like in the heat of the moment, I missed it several times and had to double back, yelling through the trees. We spent half our time hunting for equipment and the other half in a state of high-velocity frustration. We finished near the back of the pack, sore and humbled, but the lesson stuck: the team that manages scarcity the best wins the race.

THE DOUBLE CRISCO WALL

Orchard Beach, New York | October 2000 | Hi-Tec Adventure Race National Championships

One year later, my new team of David Giampietro and Steve Vadas were at the Hi-Tec National Championships at Orchard Beach, New York. We were racing as Team Never Surrender. The race director, Nick Moore, an elite adventure racer who loved the suck, started the event by giving us two ropes and requiring each team to tie their legs together. It was a three-person, four-legged race. We quickly brainstormed a solution, and we found a rhythm by having Dave in the middle chanting, "Left! Right! Left!" like a drill sergeant. We sprinted out to an early lead while other teams tripped over their own lack of coordination.

We hit the orienteering section and moved with surgical precision, thanks to my decades of navigating by paper maps. We were in second place, hunting the podium, until we hit the final obstacle: The Double Crisco Wall. It was a V-shaped plywood structure coated in a thick layer of industrial oil. We thrashed against it, slipping and failing repeatedly for what felt like an eternity. We couldn't brace ourselves to get even one man out of the pit. We were exhausted.

Eventually, the first-place team, with none other than Mike Pape, a high school buddy of mine, as captain, finished their race and came back to the trough to help pull us out. In adventure racing, you are not allowed to accept outside help, but teams are encouraged and allowed to assist one another. It was a crucial lesson: when internal resources fail, you must seek resources outside of your own unit. We took third place, stood on the podium with the big dogs, and finally had the résumé to hunt for a sponsor.

THE PERFECT POUR

Stamford, Connecticut | February 2001 | Diageo Headquarters

After spending months sending out proposals, a colleague of mine, John Boccuzzi at Bristol Technology, introduced us to a contact at Diageo, which managed a portfolio of liquor brands. In February 2001, we walked into the Diageo Headquarters in Stamford, CT. We were there to meet Leslie Arcesi, the brand manager for Guinness. Leslie agreed to a 3-year deal to sponsor the team. We strutted in acting like we owned the place, national athletes ready to sign a deal. As we sat in the boardroom, a corporate executive walked in, looked at the three of us—scruffy, bruised, and decidedly un-corporate— and asked: "So. . . where are the athletes?" That was a bit of an ego check.

We signed the deal, which would fund all of our travel, race entry fees, and new high-end racing bikes. The marketing team set up a website, sent press releases, and designed unique racing kits for us. But before the check was cut, they took us to the office bar, a full-scale replica of an Irish pub. Diageo insisted that every employee and partner know how to pour a perfect pint of Guinness. It's a two-part pour: forty-five-degree angle, let it settle, then top it off. This was my first lesson in indoctrination. You cannot sell the brand if you haven't done the work. If you don't understand the pour, you can't represent the brand.

THE DRAWSTRING LOOPHOLE

Castaic Lake, California | May 2001 | Hi-Tec Adventure Racing Series

By May, we were at Castaic Lake, California, looking like pros in our custom Guinness kits. Leslie had flown out to watch her new investment. We crushed the run and the paddle, hitting the bike transition in the lead. Then: bam. Rear-tire blowout. Steve had a flat. The tires on our new Cannondales were so tight they felt welded to the rims. What should have taken two minutes took ten. We stood on the side of the trail, red-faced, yelling at the bike and each other as teams blew past us. This is internal erosion. When you are redlined, a small friction feels like a catastrophe.

We lost the podium, and to add insult to injury, we reached the final wall only to realize we had lost our Safety String, a mandatory piece of gear we were told to hold at the start. The penalty was disqualification. I looked at our new Guinness shorts. They had a drawstring. Rip. I presented the string to the official. He smirked, but he let us pass. We finished in eighth place. We survived, but we promised Leslie we would never miss the podium again.

THE TOW LINE

To keep that promise, we had to stop relying on individual effort and start engineering a collective engine. Success in a team isn't about how fast the fastest person is; it's about the sum of the team. Dave was our fastest runner, but his speed was wasted because teams were required to stay within thirty meters of one another at all times.

We engineered a solution: the tow line.

We bought industrial shock cords and affixed them to belts. On the run, Dave literally towed Steve, transferring his surplus energy through the cord. On the kayak, Steve moved to the front boat, where he was a powerhouse, and we attached the second kayak with a cord, creating a draft line. On the bike, we hooked retractable dog leashes to the seat stems so the stronger rider could pull the weaker one.

This wasn't just a physical hack; it was a masterclass in resource allocation. The goal isn't to let the high performer win alone; it's to use their excess capacity to pull the entire unit to a higher velocity. We went on to finish first or second for the remainder of the season. We captured the overall National Series Championship trophy that year not because we were the fittest, but because we had the best math.

THE NAVIGATOR'S LOGIC

Two-Bike Math is the realization that you do not need a 1:1 ratio of tools to people to maintain 100 percent velocity. Scarcity isn't a lack of resources; it is a catalyst that forces you to engineer a Leapfrog Protocol. Scarcity is not a budget problem; it is a design challenge.

Reject the 1:1 fallacy. Most organizations wait for a full budget or perfect headcount before launching. If you have 66 percent of what you need, you have enough to start. Use rhythmic allocation to keep the mission moving. Prevent internal erosion by recognizing that when resources are low, the team's first instinct is to turn on each other. As a navigator, you must refocus that heat away from the teammates and back onto the problem.

Implement the Tow Line Strategy by identifying your surplus capacity. Transfer resources from your high performers to your bottlenecks. If one department is redlining and another has surplus energy, use a shock cord to pull the whole team forward.

THE MARKET MIRROR: SOUTHWEST AIRLINES

In the 1970s, Southwest had to sell one of its four planes to pay bills. Instead of cutting flights, they invented the 10-Minute Turn. By having everyone, including pilots, clean the cabin, they flew a four-plane schedule with three planes. They applied Two-Bike Math to aviation.

MONDAY MORNING PROTOCOLS

1. The Scarcity Drill: Identify a stalled project. Force the team to pitch a solution using half the requested budget. The innovation is hidden in the constraints.
2. The Indoctrination Pour: Mandate that every manager spends one day this quarter on the absolute front lines (customer calls or retail floor) to understand the soul of the product.
3. The Capacity Transfer: Identify your top performer and your biggest bottleneck. Attach a tow line between them, and task the top performer with systematizing their speed to pull the bottleneck forward.

Having the mathematical discipline to optimize two bikes for three people is a superpower. But once you've mastered the math of scarcity, you realize that your biggest constraint isn't money, it's time. When you are out-running the giants on a skeleton budget, the finish line is always farther than the daylight allows. It's time to face the Sleep Monster.

CHAPTER 5: THE SLEEP MONSTER

Managing Leadership through Biological Shutdown

Real-world leadership isn't about making decisions in perfect conditions; it's about remaining coherent when you are compromised. This chapter is about managing the Sleep Monster and the biological shutdown that occurs when the pressure is highest and the resources are lowest.

THE WOLF IN THE RHODODENDRONS

 "A wolf! I see a wolf!"

My teammate's voice cracked with genuine terror. I swung my headlamp toward the tree line where he was pointing. A gnarled rhododendron stump crouched in the shadows, looking exactly like a predator ready to spring. I couldn't even laugh at him. For the last hour, I had been swerving my mountain bike to avoid rabbits that weren't there.

We were deep in the Endorphin Fix, a race designed by Don Mann, a legendary Navy SEAL who didn't believe in fun runs. He believed in breaking you. We had been racing for forty hours straight. No sleep. Sixteen thousand feet of vertical gain up and down the vertical walls of the gorge. Navigating checkpoints in the West Virginia woods in daylight and in the dark. Paddling Class III and IV rapids. Rappelling off sheer cliffs. Carrying thirty pounds of gear, food, and water on our backs through the wild West Virginia forest, all without sleep.

The Sleep Monster isn't a metaphor; it is a biological shutdown. It is the moment your brain, starved of glucose and sanity, decides to rewrite reality. Around 3:00 a.m. on the second night of continuous racing is when the mask slips and the darkness reveals your soul.

My team, assembled from random participants at an adventure camp, hit a checkpoint alongside the road. We were completely cooked. We dropped to the ground, which was covered in four-inch gravel rocks, and napped for thirty minutes. They were the most comfortable rocks I had ever slept on. When we forced ourselves awake, one team member had seen enough. The lure of a warm car and a real bed was too much. He tapped out. The remaining three members rallied and committed ourselves to crossing the finish line no matter what it took. We finished in fifty-five hours with just a thirty-minute nap on the rocks.

One of the lessons away from the Endorphin Fix was that making decisions while facing the Sleep Monster is dangerous. It turns out that as terrible as you feel in the pre-dawn hours, the sunrise lifts your spirit and helps you find new energy that you didn't think you had. I made it a rule on overnight races going forward that no one quits during the night.

THE MANN PROTOCOL

Don Mann was a solid, imposing man with a standard-issue SEAL mustache and a quiet calm that masked a warrior's intensity. His own inner iron was forged in SERE school and real-world ops, including a reconnaissance mission where he had to hide in a foxhole for days, eating snakes to avoid detection. He and a SEAL teammate of his were captured once by enemy combatants and forced to bargain for their lives. When they earned their release, they swam back out into the ocean. But rather than call in for extraction, they waited until dark, then swam back into shore and continued the mission. Compared to that, a forty-eight-hour race was a vacation.

Don's mantra was simple: "Don't worry, you'll pass out before you die." There was a strange comfort in that. It gave me permission to push past my perceived limits. I realized that the redline I had lived my life under was actually miles away from the actual cliff. That newfound outlook pushed me to the finish line of the Endorphin Fix fifty-five hours after the start. It was the exact mindset I needed when I decided to drag that chaos out of the woods and into the business world.

THE VIEW FROM THE WINDOW

My office window was a frame for a life I wasn't living. I would stare at the woods, watching the way the light hit the trees, and feel a physical ache to be out in the dirt. At the time, adventure racing was my obsession—the mud, the exhaustion, the total immersion in the elements. But the Navigator in me was locked in a cage of fluorescent lights and spreadsheets. I was a man of two worlds: one driven by an entrepreneurial fire that refused to die, and the other anchored by the heavy, honorable reality of a mortgage, a wife, and two young children who relied on my stable paycheck for their survival.

Leaving wasn't a casual choice. It was a high-stakes calculation where the variables were my family's safety versus my own soul.

Then came the morning of September 11.

The world didn't just change; it shattered. For me, the tragedy wasn't a distant news cycle. I had sales clients in the World Trade Center and visited frequently. A week later, I stood on the fire escape of my colleague's office adjacent to the site. The air was still thick with the scent of pulverized concrete and lost potential. Standing there, looking at the void where those towers had been, the safety of my corporate job suddenly felt like a dangerous illusion.

I realized then that stability is often just a polite word for stagnation. The mortgage and the bills were real, but the fragility of life was more real. If the end could come that quickly, I couldn't afford to spend another Monday morning wishing I was on the other side of the glass. The events of that year didn't just push me toward a new path; they kicked me into high gear. I decided to stop staring at the woods and start walking into them, leaving the safety of the harbor to find the friction I was built for.

THE KAYAK CRISIS

Southbury, Connecticut | April 2002 | Garage Office

In early 2002, I quit my software sales job to launch Genesis Adventures. I had convinced my wife, then pregnant with our third child, that I could make a living promoting and running races. I had 40 teams signed up for my inaugural event in two days. As the race director, I had to supply the kayaks. And I had zero kayaks.

I had ordered fifty several weeks in advance, but the shipment was delayed. When I called the supplier, they casually told me they wouldn't arrive in time, as if it wasn't a big deal. I was staring at reputational ruin. I collapsed into my chair, the crushing weight of imposter syndrome pinning me down. I lost many hours of sleep that week.

Then I remembered Don Mann: "Adapt or die." I went into manual acquisition mode, driving to every sporting goods store in Connecticut to buy inflatable kayaks. I could only find fifteen. The math didn't work, so I engineered a special test. I split the teams into three groups and sent them on the run, bike, and paddle legs in a different order. On race day, I projected 100 percent certainty that this was the plan all along. The bug turned into a feature; the teams were excited to have different journeys. The race was a success because I refused to let the Sleep Monster of panic dictate the outcome.

THE HUMBLING IN THE MAINE WOODS

Backwoods, Maine | May 2003 | Appalachian Extreme 3-Day Adventure Race

By May 2003, I was leading a 225-mile expedition through the backcountry of Maine. My ego was driving the bus. My teammates, collegiate cross-country ski coaches, were praising my navigation calls. We crossed a stream to locate a checkpoint and could tell by the fact that there were no other footprints in the mud that we were in first place.

Then the Sleep Monster crept in. I made a bad call at a fork in a poorly mapped fire road. We headed down the wrong path for almost an hour until we unexpectedly hit a paved road. The realization that we were miles off track was a gut punch. In adventure racing, you don't guess your way back. You have to swallow your pride and retrace your steps to the last certain point on the map.

The mistake had cost us precious hours that would catch up to us. Later that night, we were hiking our bikes under a set of powerlines searching for the next checkpoint, which had a time cutoff. We pushed on as long as we could through the night, hoping to find our destination just over the next ridge. Exhausted and defeated, we collapsed in a patch of green grass for a nap. When we woke up, it was a horror movie. We found one tick. Then another. Then dozens. We had to strip naked in the freezing Maine air, picking insects off every inch of our skin. Nature doesn't care about your ego. If you lose focus for one second, the woods will eat you alive. We missed the time cutoff and had to ride our bikes on a short course to the finish line.

When you are under the spell of the Sleep Monster, you have to adjust your decision making. You have to check your ego, rely on your teammates and sometimes, simply decide that sleep is the best option.

THE ANOMALY FROM MANHATTAN

Ringwood State Park, New Jersey | June 2003 | Genesis Adventure Race

The two mountain bikers would not have seemed out of place normally, but they were riding into the park on the road and looked disheveled. I recognized one of the guys immediately. He had attended the very first Genesis race in Connecticut and returned a few more times with his brother. He introduced me to his riding partner. "Brian, I'd like to introduce you to Joe De Sena." I had heard Joe's name floated in the adventure racing circles, but this was my first time meeting him in person.

The duo had ridden their bikes from Lower Manhattan all night just to get to the race. The Sleep Monster was starting to set in.

"We didn't register," he said, handing me a wad of sweaty cash from his pocket. "And we don't have a map or any equipment."

I handed them instructions and spare life jackets. They shoved off with a level of confidence that bordered on the absurd. I had a strange feeling that I might not see them again.

The race day went on without too much drama until the early afternoon. A staff member radioed me: "I have a racer reporting possible human remains in the woods." I thought the report was a bit absurd, but it was Northern New Jersey and a *Sopranos* moment was not entirely out of the question. I raced to the coordinates, heart pounding, only to find a deer carcass. It was the first time in the woods for some of the NYC crowd.

By sunset we were packing up our equipment. Joe's team was still missing. I jumped on my bike and took off into the woods. I eventually found them pedaling along a gas pipeline deep in the park. They weren't stressed. They weren't broken. They were already discussing the forty-mile ride back to the city that night. They would be on the go for over thirty hours straight. Joe's navigation was lacking, but his engine was top-notch. The spark had met the gasoline.

THE NAVIGATOR'S LOGIC

The Sleep Monster is the voice of the rational mind begging you to quit, settle, or compromise. Real-world leadership is about fatigue management, building a team that remains coherent when every individual is redlined. When your mind tells you that you are finished, you are actually only at about 40 percent of your capacity. As Don Mann proved, the perceived redline is usually miles away from the actual cliff.

Never make a permanent decision in a temporary state of exhaustion. The dawn has a magical way of rewriting the narrative, but in the dark, you are a victim of your own chemistry.

When the shipment of kayaks doesn't arrive, your team needs a navigator, not a mourner. Projecting 100 percent confidence buys you the time and the trust required to engineer a workaround.

THE MARKET MIRROR: APOLLO 13

On the Apollo 13 mission when the oxygen tank exploded, NASA didn't have the kayaks they needed. Gene Kranz enforced the No Quitting rule, forcing engineers to build a filter out of plastic bags and duct tape while freezing and sleep-deprived. They solved the problem while compromised by creating a makeshift CO_2 scrubber using only what was available on the ship. They didn't have the luxury of perfect conditions; they had to engineer in the dark.

MONDAY MORNING PROTOCOLS

1. Establish the Darkness Rule: No major strategic pivots or personnel firings after 5:00 p.m. or at the end of a grueling sprint. Wait for dawn to calibrate your chemistry.
2. The Don Mann Stress Test: Run a thirty-minute tabletop exercise assuming your biggest operational fear has already happened. Engineer the workaround before the crisis hits to prevent panic.
3. The Code Audit: Reward the next person who publicly owns a failure. Build a culture where people run back up the mountain to fix mistakes they could have easily hidden, reinforcing the integrity of the map.

Navigating the Sleep Monster proves that your team has the grit to endure the darkness. But pure endurance eventually hits a wall of systemic chaos and unsolvable messes. To maintain your velocity, you need more than just a team that suffers together; you need the individual who is willing to step out from behind the shield wall and absorb the spears alone. Sometimes, to save the mission, someone has to be willing to take the hit. It's time to identify the sacrificial lamb.

CHAPTER 6: THE SACRIFICIAL LAMB

Absorbing Systemic Friction to Save the Mission

In every high-growth surge, there is a moment where the system fails. To keep the mission alive, someone must be willing to be the anchor, absorbing the friction of the mistake so the team can keep moving toward the finish line.

THE LAMB

Hither Hills State Park, Long Island | September 2004 |
Corporate Adventure Race

Fifty Wall Street desk jockeys were staring up at a gray-haired
man giving the opening remarks to the Trekkin' in the
Hamptons adventure race. Two luxury buses hummed in the
otherwise deserted parking lot. Up on a guard rail stood a tall,
gray-haired man talking through a bullhorn, pumping up the
crowd.

The scene was much bigger than expected, and the crowd
was a magnet for attention. Then, through a gap in the trees, I
saw the flash of a New York state trooper cruiser. My blood
pressure spiked because I knew this was going to be trouble.
My body went cold with a sudden, sharp adrenaline chill as the
cruiser made a U-turn and headed straight for us. I didn't have
a permit.

THE "JOE'D" PHENOMENON

Earlier that year, Joe De Sena had reached out after a year of
silence. He wanted me to organize an adventure race for his
corporate clients. When I contacted the park office, they told
me the event was too small for a permit. Joe had told me he
expected ten to fifteen people. But I had been Joe'd. Being
Joe'd is what happens when Joe's think-big mentality collides
with the laws of physics. Forty-eight hours before the start, he
nonchalantly mentioned the headcount was fifty. To Joe, this
was a massive success. To me, it meant we were now
operating in arrestable territory with a forty-foot truck and a
fleet of kayaks.

"Send them now!" I shouted to the man with the megaphone.
"Get them in the woods now!" The emcee on the fence quickly
wrapped up his speech and yelled "GO!" The crowd scrambled

into the trees just as the trooper pulled up. I jumped into my truck to head over to the kayaking section on the other side of the woods, worried that we were about to be shut down. Fortunately, the man with the microphone was uniquely qualified for a standoff.

THE BINNS MANEUVER

The man addressing the crowd was Jimmy Binns, a Philadelphia legal legend who had represented Muhammad Ali and played the boxing commissioner in the Rocky movies. He carried a specific kind of high-trust authority that you can't manufacture. Jimmy Binns didn't hesitate. He stepped directly into the officer's path, acting as a fault-tolerance system. He used his status not to avoid the conflict, but to absorb it. He treated the trooper like an opponent at a boxing weigh-in, buying us the time we needed by becoming the lead sink for the officer's attention. The trooper eventually arrested him. Binns didn't flinch. He took the ride to the station, argued the law on the way, and was issued several fines. By the time the final racers crossed the line, he was back at the event, perfectly composed, handing out medals. Jimmy was our *sacrificial lamb*. He understood that the event must reach completion; the litigation happens in the background.

THE LOST TRADERS

While Jimmy was in a holding cell, the participants were blissfully unaware of the chaos. They paddled, biked, and ran toward the Montauk Lighthouse. Then they hit a final three-mile beach run to the finish line. We waited at the finish line, but one team was missing. We had no idea how anyone could get lost. You just had to follow the ocean. We started to form a search party. Finally, they appeared, strolling down the beach with cigarettes in one hand and cocktails in the other. "Where were you?" I asked, exasperated. "We saw a nice bar," one trader shrugged. "So we stopped." Lesson learned: Not everyone races for the podium. Some people race for the open bar.

THE TRIATHLETE PIZZA OVEN

Harriman State Park, NY | May 2006 | Harryman Half Iron Triathlon

Two years later, I faced a different kind of systemic failure. The Harryman Triathlon was underway in forty-degree rain. Suddenly, five police cruisers screamed into the parking lot with sirens blaring. "Where are the bodies?" an officer yelled. They were responding to a mass casualty incident (MCI). In the emergency world, an MCI is reserved for plane crashes or terrorist attacks. The reality? A bunch of spandex-wearing triathletes were shivering in the rain.

When the combined water and air temperature totals below 100, hypothermia is inevitable. Racers were hitting the downhill bike section at thirty miles per hour, soaking wet, and shutting down. They were pulling over to ask park police for help one by one. Because the police were on a separate radio network with an automatic escalation protocol, the system saw a mass casualty event instead of a cold race. In our medical tent, we were shoving shivering bodies into an ambulance with the heater on max, it looked like a triathlete pizza oven. Our lead medic, who worked for the port authority, stepped up as the sacrificial lamb. He de-escalated the police and absorbed the procedural friction. From that day on, we gave the police our own radios. Communication is the only antidote to chaos.

THE DEATH RACE AND THE HARD RESET

While I was refining Genesis Adventures, Joe was turning his farm in Pittsfield, Vermont, into a laboratory for suffering. He created the Death Race—an unstructured torture chamber where people paid to translate Greek dictionaries, lug rocks, and eat bags of raw onions. It was the ultimate search for the system floor. By 2008, I had the systems and Joe had the chaos. But the Great Recession was about to execute a market-wide system halt. The era of expensive, boutique adventure races was over. We didn't know it yet, but the market was begging us to package this resilience for the masses. We needed to solve for volume.

THE NAVIGATOR'S LOGIC

In an adventure race, participants are always pushing the boundaries of what is allowed. Obtaining clarification of the rules can limit your options. Sometimes you have to act as the sacrificial lamb to force the system to update its rules. You can fix a messy launch; you cannot fix a launch that never happened.

Identify the anchor. In moments of systemic fragility, identify the person or department who can absorb the legal or operational shock. Let them hold the line while the rest of the organization maintains its vector.

Momentum is a weapon: markets react to motion. Once the train is moving, obstacles, whether they are permits or competitors, tend to move out of the way or negotiate with the momentum. Bridge the communication gap: disconnected networks create mass casualty scares in business. Ensure your internal logic is translated for external authorities like regulators, boards, or police before the friction hits.

THE MARKET MIRROR: AIRBNB

Airbnb knew that asking for permission in New York City would allow the hotel lobby to crush them. They chose to launch, achieve social gravity, and treat regulatory fines as a customer acquisition cost. They absorbed the friction to protect the revolution, realizing that by the time the regulations caught up, the community would already be too large to ignore.

MONDAY MORNING PROTOCOLS

1. The Catastrophe Filter: Look at tasks waiting for approval. If executing without permission won't land you in jail or bankruptcy, execute one today. Do not ask.
2. The Default-to-Yes Policy: If a manager doesn't reply to an approval request within twenty-four hours, the answer is automatically yes.
3. The Flash Fire Drill: Launch a twenty-four-hour initiative with zero notice today. Watch where the team stumbles; this reveals your mobilization friction.

You've learned to absorb the spears to save the mission. But as the world's economy began to fracture in 2007 and 2008, we realized that boutique adventure races were a luxury, and survival was about to become a mass-market necessity. It was time to stop running events and start building a movement. To do that, we had to move from the shadows of the woods to the center of the town square.

THE FORGE MANIFESTO: THE STANDARD IS THE STRATEGY

Navigator's Note: In ancient Greece, the Phalanx was a dense, impenetrable formation of infantry. Every soldier held a shield that protected not just himself, but the man to his left. If one person broke rank, the entire wall failed. In business, your Phalanx is the core team that operates as a single, unbreakable unit—where individual egos are sacrificed for collective survival.

You have exited the woods of the origin story. You have seen how the suck was refined on the Vermont farm and the hallucination-filled trails of West Virginia. But you haven't just been reading a history; you have been undergoing a recalibration.

To move into the market, you must carry the Four Laws of the Forge with you:

1. You no longer hire for bullet points on a page; you hire for the resilience filter. You seek the believers who can handle the sand in their shoes without losing their stride. A résumé tells you what a person has done; the Phalanx tells you who they will become when the friction starts. You are not building a staff; you are interlocking shields with people who refuse to let the line break.
2. The Azimuth over the Permission: You stop waiting for the establishment to clear the road. You find the stealth vector, look for the path the rules didn't see, and move while your competitors are still asking for clarification.

3. The Scrappiness over the Budget: You embrace Two-Bike Math. You stop waiting for a 1:1 ratio of resources to people. Scarcity isn't a handicap; it's the fuel for innovation.
4. The Baseline over the Comfort: You have recalibrated what hard feels like. You know that the Sleep Monster is a liar and that your true capacity is miles beyond where your brain tells you to quit.

You are no longer a spectator of the struggle. You are the architect of it. The forge is cold. The weapon is sharp.

END OF PART I: THE FORGE

You are no longer just a collection of individuals; you are a unit forged for the friction.

You possess the Ancestry of Grit and the internal baseline to survive anything the wilderness throws at you. But a weapon sitting in a rack achieves nothing. All those years of freezing in the Vermont mud and calculating vectors in the pool were just the apprenticeship.

It is time to take these principles and strike the market. The world is about to meet Spartan.

PART II: THE SPARK

The Engineering of Momentum and the Logic of Global Proliferation

---

Scaling a movement is not about enlarging a single success; it is about deconstructing that success into a deployable standard. Before Spartan was a global institution, it was a logistical war, a decade-long deployment where the goal was to flat-pack the suck and ship it to forty countries. In "The Spark," you learn that a brand's true power is found in its repeatability. If you cannot translate your raw intensity into a system that functions while you sleep, you are not building a legacy; you are just managing a series of expensive accidents. Real growth occurs when the pirate energy of the forge meets the precision of the blueprint.

Most organizations mistake safety for survival. In a hyper-growth window, a fortress of seed capital and a year-long planning cycle are actually forms of *lethal friction*. Success belongs to the team that can process reality faster than the incumbent can hold a committee meeting.

THE OODA LOOP: INSIDE THE DOGFIGHT

Velocity is your primary protection. If you move fast enough, the spears of market friction will miss you. In the military, this is known as the OODA Loop, a concept developed by Colonel John Boyd.

Boyd, a legendary fighter pilot, used this model to explain how a pilot in a technically inferior plane could still win a dogfight. It wasn't about who had the faster jet; it was about who had the shorter cycle between an idea and the dirt.

This is the loop:

1. **Observe:** Collect raw data by scanning the environment and the competition.
2. **Orient:** Make sense of the chaos based on your experience and mental models.
3. **Decide:** Select the fastest effective course of action.
4. **Act:** Execute immediately.

In 2010, the jet we were flying was a startup with no employees, no office, and no permits. Our competitors like Warrior Dash and Tough Mudder had better planes. But we were about to get inside their loop.

THE TERADYNE VECTOR: ASSEMBLY FRICTION

My understanding of the OODA Loop didn't start in the mud; it started in a cubicle. My first job out of college was software programming at Teradyne, a Fortune 500 company obsessed with Total Quality Management (TQM). They built massive, multi-million-dollar testing equipment for the semiconductor industry. At that level, friction isn't just an annoyance; it's a line item that can bankrupt a firm.

The company put every employee on a cross-functional quality team and cut them loose to eliminate waste. Within this context I learned about the Pareto Effect. By laying out data in different views, the goal was to get one or problem to stand out more than the others. You fixed that problem first, then moved on to the next.

One team deconstructed the assembly of their massive testers and the largest count of parts was the bolts to hold the machine together. They found over fifty different types of bolts used in a single machine. Every unique bolt required a different tool, a different bin, and a different procurement path. The mechanical engineers on the team had a new perspective. They redesigned the unit down to just ten fasteners. They didn't just save time; they cleared an entire floor of inventory space.

PARALLEL INTEGRATION: CRUSHING THE CYCLE

Teradyne's customers were goliaths like Intel and Motorola who were churning out cutting-edge technology as fast as they could. In the semiconductor testing world, time is the only currency. You have to test tomorrow's technology with yesterday's equipment. If you fall behind, you die.

As we launched the project for next-generation testers, we realized a linear process, where Hardware Engineering handed off to Software Engineering who handed off to Manufacturing, who handed off to Shipping, was a relic. We blew it up in favor of parallel integration.

We took one person from every functional group, from the lead coder to the person responsible for the final shipping crate, and put them on one team from Day 1. The person packaging the tester had upfront input on the design, ensuring the product didn't need to be redesigned later just to fit on a truck.

By closing the loop between departments, we crushed a five-year process into under two. I learned then that speed is a function of integration. If you wait for the hand-off, you have already lost the race.

THE SPARTAN REALITY

By the time Joe and I decided to light the fuse on Spartan, the market was already moving. Warrior Dash and ToughMudder were scaling. If we had waited until we were ready—renting an office, hiring a C-suite, and writing one-hundred-page SOPs (standard operating procedures)—we would have been irrelevant.

A normal company would have spent $1,000,000 and 365 days building a fortress of safety. By choosing the spark over the fortress, we saved a million dollars and gained something far more valuable: the market. We observed their slow, linear movements, oriented ourselves to the gap, decided to move forward with 66% of the resources and acted before they could gain more traction.

We are moving into the era of hyper-growth. The rules of the wilderness still apply, but the stakes are now measured in burn rates, market share, and global scale.

Welcome to the dogfight. It's time to turn the loop.

CHAPTER 7: THE COFFEE SHOP COUP

Complexity Is Often a Sophisticated Form of Procrastination

This chapter is about how a single napkin and a spite-driven vision ignited a category-defining movement before the first permit was even signed.

Hartford, Connecticut | December 2009 | Coffee Shop

The birthplace of a global movement wasn't a sleek innovation lab or a high-rise boardroom. It was a sterile, fluorescent-lit coffee shop off I-84 that felt perpetually ten minutes away from closing. It was just a collection of wobbly tables with silver legs and a lingering chill. I was leaning across the table, arguing with a maniac.

"That won't work! You can't get massive throughput with a mini-Death Race concept," I said. "It's logistically impossible."

Joe De Sena didn't blink. He was en route from New York to Vermont and had pulled off the highway to meet me. He brought Sean McGuire and one of his traders from his firm. I sat there watching the Tasmanian Devil of Wall Street spin in front of me, trying to assess if this was a project already in motion or the raw genesis of a hallucination. It was clearly the latter.

THE SUICIDAL TIMELINE

Joe leaned in, his eyes wide with that specific brand of fire-breather intensity that ignores the laws of gravity. "Okay, fine. If the Death Race doesn't scale, figure out something else. And I want ten of them."

I did the mental math. It was December 26. "Ten races in 2011?" I asked.

"No," Joe shot back. "2010."

I slumped back into my seat. We were five days away from the New Year. This was the first real moment of friction between Joe's fire and my physics since the Hamptons. He wasn't asking for a race; he was asking for a miracle. I had been producing events for ten years at this point. I knew the sheer logistical weight required to move a mountain: permits, insurance, venues, marketing, and staff. To launch one major event in twelve months is a sprint. To launch ten, starting in five days, is suicide.

"Who is leading this project?" I asked, assuming there was a hidden army already at work.

Silence. Everyone looked around the table. Sean owned a bar in Manhattan; the trader had a full-time day job, as did Joe. I was the only one at the table with the expertise, the time, and frankly, the insanity to get this done. I pulled a thin, white napkin from the dispenser. Joe grabbed my blue Bic pen. Over that wobbly table, Spartan was forged. The philosophy of leveraging friction moved from theory to a concrete business plan: "$100,000, Mini Death Race, 10 Events in 2010."

THE RED FROG REBUFF

Joe's motivation wasn't just ambition; it was revenge. Weeks earlier, he had visited the headquarters of Red Frog Events in Chicago, the creators of Warrior Dash. They were the kings of the hill, popping over two thousand people per event, with guys in Viking helmets and turkey legs.

Joe had offered them a deal: a feeder system for his elite Death Race. The kids at Red Frog laughed him out of the office. They were selling fun; they didn't need intensity. Joe walked out of that office and decided to build his own mountain. He didn't want to compete with them; he wanted to bury them. My struggle was internalizing Joe's spite while trying to calculate the vector of how we'd actually survive it. Joe wanted the horizon to start yesterday. I was the one who had to make sure the ground didn't disappear beneath us.

BECOMING SPARTAN ONE

As I drove home to Florida, I felt the friction of the safe path. I was considering becoming a school teacher, the safe option. A steady paycheck, summer vacations, and predictability. It was logical. It was honorable. But it felt like a slow death. I realized that if I took the teaching job, I would be trading possibility for security. Joe's offer wasn't a contract; it was a treasure map. We had zero brand, zero venues, and almost zero time. But we had a clear target.

I decided to bet on the chaos. While Joe was patient zero, the visionary who lit the fuse, we reached an agreement, and I officially became **Spartan One**. I was the first one through the door, the navigator tasked with turning a napkin sketch into a global team. Joe was adamant: his capital went strictly toward the race build and marketing—no heavy overhead, no fat salaries. We agreed on a pirate package: a small monthly retainer and a revenue share on future ticket sales. The calculus was simple: If nobody came, I starved. If the movement exploded, I won.

OUTRUNNING THE INFRASTRUCTURE

The $100,000 napkin deal wasn't a safety net; it was a gas can. It required us to outrun our own infrastructure at a pace that felt less like growth and more like a fever dream. The task list was a monstrous, living organism, growing heads faster than we could cut them off. The struggle between Joe's "more, faster" and my drive for systematic scale was a constant, low-frequency hum. He'd call with a new idea that defied the laws of physics and the constraints of the budget; I'd have to find the azimuth to make it work without the whole machine seizing up. We were building the plane while it was in a vertical dive, except we were still mining the ore to make the wings.

It started with the dirt. I spent my days on the phone, convincing skeptical landowners to let us dig trenches and run thousands of mud-caked strangers through their private sanctuaries. I had to sell them on a vision that sounded, to any sane person, like a liability nightmare. We weren't just renting a field; we were negotiating for the right to temporarily destroy it. Fortunately, I found a guy who had raced a Genesis adventure race previously, and he worked at a cross-country ski facility in Vermont. He was down for the new concept.

Once the land was secured, we had to design obstacles that occupied the razor-thin gap between legal and lethal. They had to be safe enough to satisfy the corporate lawyers and insurance agents but hard enough to break the spirit of a professional athlete. We were sourcing industrial-grade lumber, miles of barbed wire, and heavy-gauge steel. We weren't just building structures; we were building the physical manifestations of the brand. If a wall failed, the company died.

You can't have a movement without a crowd, and a crowd doesn't just appear in a remote Vermont field by accident. We built a website and a Facebook page. We were hacking the early Facebook algorithm, turning every like into a social endorsement. We were still licking stamps on physical mailers, sending out glossy postcards that promised a life-changing experience to people who hadn't even heard of obstacle racing yet. We weren't just selling tickets; we were building a database of the brave.

Then came the high-stakes math of life and death. You can't run a high-risk event without a medical plan. I was on the phone with EMTs, flight nurses, and emergency physicians, trying to explain that we needed a mobile field hospital in the middle of a Vermont cow pasture. We had to coordinate with local food vendors to keep the masses fed and source water to keep them hydrated. We were calculating water intake per racer without knowing how many were going to show up. It was a logistics puzzle where the pieces were human lives.

We needed waivers that didn't read like death warrants and were trying to find an insurance company insane enough to cover us. We were a Death Race brand seeking standard commercial liability. It was a paradox. Every yes from an underwriter felt like a stay of execution. We were building a massive logistical engine: T-shirts, medals, water tankers, timing chips, while the bank account fluctuated like a heart rate in a sprint.

THE NAVIGATOR'S LOGIC

Most businesses die in the analysis phase because they are waiting for a green light that never comes. The friction advantage requires you to attack before you are ready. You don't build a movement by being reasonable; you build it by declaring war on the average.

Attack the hesitation. Waiting for 100 percent data is a death sentence. In a high-velocity environment, a 66 percent plan executed with 100 percent audacity wins because it generates real-world feedback while the competition is still stuck in a meeting.

Burn the boats. Make a public or financial commitment that makes retreat impossible. Once the date is announced and the resources are spent, the only way out is through.

Identify the niche wedge. Find where the market leader is indifferent to their customers. Warrior Dash was selling fun. We sold transformation through suffering. By attacking the space they were too soft to occupy, we created a gravity well they couldn't escape.

THE MARKET MIRROR: DOLLAR SHAVE CLUB

In 2012, Gillette owned the market with massive R&D and complex retail relationships. Dollar Shave Club didn't try to out-engineer them; they used spite-driven simplicity. With a single viral video and a napkin-simple subscription model, they attacked where the giant was indifferent to the customer's wallet. They didn't build a fortress; they ignited a spark that forced a billion-dollar acquisition. They proved that a clear, bold message can disrupt a legacy superpower that has grown complacent.

MONDAY MORNING PROTOCOLS

1. The Napkin Audit: Take your current fifty-page business plan or project brief and force yourself to distill it onto a single napkin or a 3 x 5 card. If you cannot explain the niche wedge—the one thing you do that the market leader is too slow or too soft to do—you are hiding in complexity.
2. The Spite Assessment: Identify one competitor who has grown fat and happy. Where have they stopped listening to their customers? That indifference is your entry point. Attack that specific gap with 100 percent audacity this week.

The Coffee Shop Coup gave us the fire. But a napkin isn't a race course, and spite isn't a logistical plan. To move from a spark to a reality, we had to enter a five-month deep-work phase where theory would meet the cold reality of the spreadsheet. It was time for the prototype test, the grueling countdown where we had to engineer the DNA of a new category before the first starting cannon ever fired.

CHAPTER 8: THE PROTOTYPE TEST

Designing for Durability through Rapid Iteration

If your organization waits for a perfect plan to move, you've already lost the frequency. Real growth doesn't come from a boardroom blueprint; it comes from throwing a rough draft against a wall and seeing where it cracks. The ultimate test of your brand's durability isn't how well you plan, but how fast you can iterate.

THE 300 WORKOUT

Vero Beach, Florida | January 2010 | Workout Failure

"Dang, it's still taking me over thirty minutes, and I can't finish the pull-ups."

I was venting to my brother-in-law, Greg Cavoli. Greg was a fitness fanatic, the kind of guy who scoured the internet for the hardest challenges he could find. His latest obsession was the 300 Workout.

This was the legendary regimen created by Mark Twight to forge the bodies of the actors for the movie *300*. It wasn't just a workout; it was a soul-crusher.

- 25 pull-ups
- 50 deadlifts
- 50 push-ups
- 50 box jumps
- 50 floor wipers
- 50 clean-and-presses
- 25 pull-ups
- Total reps: 300.
- Rest: none

This obsession was bubbling in the background during the lead-up to the Hartford meeting. It was Spartan in its purest form, a raw friction advantage born not in a boardroom, but in the sweat and failure of a garage gym.

We had five months to build a national series from scratch. We had the mechanics (obstacles), but we lacked the mythology.

As we brainstormed names, I mentioned the 300 Workout. That single reference point led us directly to **Spartan.** The moment the word hit the table, the project changed. We weren't just organizing an event; we were tapping into 2,500 years of history. We had imagery, a philosophy, and a backstory. We weren't just putting on races; we were creating a modern Agoge. Joe was already recruiting others to join the fledgling team.

Pittsfield, Vermont | January 2010 | Status: The Prototype Test

Joe's farm in Vermont was a vortex. It sat right off the Long Trail, the oldest long-distance hiking path in the US and the inspiration for the Appalachian Trail. That trail brought a specific type of person to the farm: nomadic, resilient, and willing to work for food. Joe had a standing offer: lodging and meals in exchange for manual labor. Two of those hikers, Richard (a sharp-witted Brit) and Selica (a savvy Montrealer), walked into Joe's life and never left. They became Spartans 2 and 3. They lived on the farm and worked in the sweatbox office. They were the first Phalanx, a team built on proximity and grit rather than résumés. But as the navigator, I knew that more people meant more friction, and our first collision was over the very soul of the brand.

THE BATTLE OF THE SUFFIX

The identity of the company was forged on a chaotic conference call that felt like a diplomatic standoff. I was on one side; Richard and Selica were on the other. Joe was the silent listener in the background, likely yelling at traders on another line. The fight was over a single word.

"We should call it the Spartan Run or Spartan Challenge," Richard argued. "The word *race* scares people. It implies you have to be fast, and timing the events is too expensive."

Their logic was sound. *Challenge* was inclusive. *Run* was safe. But I stood my ground. My computer science mind demanded metrics; my competitive spirit demanded a winner. "No," I countered. "It has to be a race. Hi-Tec and Ironman were successful because they had elite athletes attracting the aspirational athletes."

A challenge has no standard; if you finish, you win. But a race introduces the most brutal form of friction known to man: the clock. The clock is an objective truth. By choosing *race*, we were betting on human nature: People say they want fun, but they crave status. They want to know exactly where they stand in the hierarchy. Joe stayed silent, letting us battle it out, but my refusal to settle won. We became **Spartan Race**.

THE FESTIVAL COMPROMISE

While I won the battle for the sport, I hit a wall on the culture. I demanded timing chips, penalties, and legitimate obstacles. I wanted a sport, not a mud run. Richard and Selica saw it differently. They wanted a medieval Woodstock. Their vision included Renaissance-style attractions, turkey legs, jousting, and flowing beer. My initial instinct was to kill it. It felt goofy. It felt like a distraction from the Death Race ethos Joe and I were trying to scale.

I looked at the board and calculated my political capital. I had already secured the timing chips and the burpees. If I fought them on the party, I risked alienating the very people Joe had empowered to build the atmosphere. I couldn't fight a two-front war. "You handle the party," I told them. "I'll handle the pain."

It was a brilliant accident. The juxtaposition of a militaristic race and a hedonistic festival created a unique dopamine loop: survive the hell, enter the heaven. We inadvertently created the work-hard, play-hard duality that became the brand's signature.

PIRATE ENGINEERING: THE OBSTACLE LAB

We had zero budget and extreme goals. We had to innovate our way through every special test. Richard and I looked at my adventure racing history as a baseline and optimized for individual suffering.

The walls (4', 6', and 8') provided scalable, vertical friction that demanded explosive power. The zig-zag balance beam was cheap to build but required a mental reset; if your heart rate is 180, you have to find your center instantly or fail. Joe brought the catalyst energy to the mud crawl, suggesting we replace the standard low string with barbed wire. Suddenly, the suck had real stakes. For the spear throw, professional spears were a luxury, so Richard took a shovel handle, glued a large nail into the tip, and pointed it at a hay bale. Pirate engineering at its finest.

THE JUNIOR PHALANX

Right from the start, I made a strategic decision: we would not leave the children behind. Most events treated kids as a nuisance to be managed in a daycare tent. We took the opposite vector, viewing the kids' race as the on-ramp for the next generation. We gave them scaled walls and their own mud crawl. The true mathematical vector of this choice revealed itself fifteen years later. The eight-year-olds who crawled through the Vermont mud in 2010 are now twenty-four-year-old elite athletes. We didn't just build a customer base; we built a biological pipeline.

THE CONFLUENCE: CROSSFIT & FACEBOOK

As we built the product, two massive waves crashed together in the American psyche. The CrossFit catalyst had already taught a massive demographic the language of capability.

They were training for the unknown and unknowable in garages, and we provided the pro day. Simultaneously, we hit the Facebook golden era. In 2010, organic reach was 100 percent. We decided to give photos away for free. When a racer tagged themselves jumping over fire, it blasted into the newsfeeds of their five hundred friends. One racer became a billboard for five hundred prospects. Joe saw this digital leverage before anyone. While other CEOs were buying billboards, Joe was handing his credit card to interns and saying, "Buy the clicks."

THE NAVIGATOR'S LOGIC

The most dangerous friction in a new project is legacy thinking. To gain a velocity advantage, you must use the blank page to prototype the bolts of your business from scratch.

Words matter. A challenge is a commodity; a race is a hierarchy. If you want to build a tribe, give them a way to measure their status against each other.

You cannot fight every battle, so learn the 70/30 compromise. I protected the pain (the race) and ceded the party (the festival), creating a brand duality that appealed to both the athlete and the weekend warrior.

Don't just market to the current generation; build the biological pipeline. Create an on-ramp for the next one. If you can change a child's baseline for what hard looks like, you own that customer for life.

THE MARKET MIRROR: SPACEX

SpaceX famously embraces rapid iteration. Instead of spending a decade designing the perfect rocket on paper, they build prototypes and fly them until they explode. Each failure provides real-world data: structural vibrations, engine heat, telemetry glitches, that a simulation could never produce. They engineer their DNA through the suck of real-world testing, moving closer to the goal with every charred launch pad. They prove that in innovation, velocity is the best defense against obsolescence.

MONDAY MORNING PROTOCOLS

1. The Shovel Handle Solution: Identify a project that is stalled because you are waiting for a high-cost professional tool or service. Force your team to build a pirate engineering version today, a low-cost, functional prototype that allows you to start testing the logic immediately. Perfection is the enemy of the first one hundred customers.
2. The Suffix Test: Audit your brand language. Are you selling a challenge (a commodity) or a race (a hierarchy)? Introduce a way for your customers to measure themselves against an objective standard. Humans crave status; give them the clock and watch the engagement skyrocket.

The prototype test proved we could codify the grit. We had the name, the venue, and the digital advertising vector primed. But in the early days of a revolution, algorithms are useless at creating believers. Joe had the vision, I had the system, but now we needed the boots on the ground crazy enough to march into the fire. It was time to recruit the raiders.

CHAPTER 9: DORM ROOM RAIDERS

Marketing is traditionally viewed as a trade of capital for eyeballs. But in a hyper-growth window, capital is too slow and eyeballs are too flighty. You don't need a marketing budget; you need social gravity—the manufactured force that makes your brand feel inevitable.

THE INTERLOPERS

Middlebury College Campus, VT | March 2010 | The Quad

Matt and Ben picked up their pace. They had been spotted. On their tail was a campus police officer looking at them suspiciously. They looked the part, freshly out of college, wearing jeans and heavy pullover sweatshirts. They had been roaming the campus all day, infiltrating the library and slipping into dormitories, but as they crossed the quad toward one final building, the law of consequences caught up to them.

"Hey, you guys!" shouted the guard.

Matt and Ben continued to walk, pretending the wind had swallowed the call. But the guard accelerated, closing the gap. "Do you fellows go to school here?" he asked firmly. They thought for a moment about lying, but their IDs clearly said Castleton College. They admitted they were outsiders and were ordered to leave immediately. They retreated to their car, adrenaline pumping. They hadn't stolen anything; they had just committed guerrilla marketing: the scrappy art of using surprise and unconventional tactics to hijack the public's attention without a massive budget.

THE NERVE CENTER (THE YOGA STUDIO)

The nerve center of the Spartan revolution was a contradiction in terms. The office for Peak Adventures, Joe's event business in Vermont (Spartan Race would be created later), was tucked into the back of a converted house that served as the town's yoga studio. Rule number one: no shoes on the golden pine floor. You had to walk across that pristine, Zen floor to get to the back, where two glass doors led to the trading floor. Inside, the vibe shifted from Namaste to *Wolf of Wall Street*. Two desks were crammed with eight monitors each, flickering with high-frequency trades.

And then there was Joe. He rigged a high desk with a stationary bike as his chair. He would sit there, pedaling miles to nowhere, sweat dripping onto the floor, screaming about obstacle designs while executing millions in trades. This was the environment Matt and Ben walked into. They were looking for an internship; they found a war room.

THE MISSION: 10,000 LIKES

Their first goal was simple: "Get the Spartan Facebook page to ten thousand likes by Friday or you're fired." In 2010, we leveraged a fundamental law of human physics: nothing attracts a crowd like a crowd. If people see an empty restaurant, they keep walking. If they see a line out the door, they join it.

Richard, our British tech wizard, handed the boys a stack of cash and a snippet of JavaScript code. The mission was to go to college campuses, find students with laptops, and give them five dollars to run the script. The script was a suggestion engine that instantly invited every friend on that student's list to like the Spartan page. Back home, I sat at my computer, hitting Refresh. Plus fifty. Plus one hundred. Seeing that digital odometer spin was addictive. We were weaponizing social pressure to create the appearance of a movement before we had a single obstacle in the ground.

THE JOE STARE

Matt and Ben returned to Pittsfield feeling like conquering heroes. They walked into the General Store, the town hub Joe had purchased, and Matt slammed the remaining cash onto the table with emphatic swagger. He wanted to prove he was a killer salesman who didn't even need the bribe money to close the deal. They had convinced dozens of students to open their Facebook pages and tell all of their friends to Like the Spartan page. He expected a high-five. Instead, he got the Joe Stare. Joe looked at the cash, then at Matt.

"Why do you still have this money?"

To Joe, saving resources was a lack of ambition. In the Spartan phalanx, efficiency is a secondary metric, volume is king. If you had cash left, it meant you hadn't pushed the line far enough. My struggle as the navigator was constantly trying to keep the wheels on the bus while Joe was trying to pour more gasoline into the engine. He wanted more leads, more noise, and more chaos. I wanted a system that wouldn't bankrupt us.

THE FABRICATED REALITY

We had ten thousand likes, but zero photos of a real race for our website. So, we faked it. Richard and Selica staged a photoshoot on the farm during mud season. It was freezing, but you can't see temperature in a JPEG. They gathered everyone they could find: traders, farmhands, locals. They set up makeshift obstacles and shot everything at tight angles to make fifteen people look like a packed crowd. We were selling a reality that didn't exist yet, capitalizing on the fact that no one actually knew what an obstacle race was supposed to look like. We were building credibility out of thin air and pixels.

THE MONTREAL FLANK

As the calendar moved toward our first event, Selica dropped a bomb: "Let's do the second race in Montreal."

I fought it immediately. The friction between Joe's urge to expand everywhere and my need to navigate one mile at a time hit a flashpoint. "We haven't even finished the first event!" I argued. "We have customs, currency exchange, and a French website. It's insane." But as we debated, the strategic fog lifted. Warrior Dash was stuck in the US. If we crossed the border first, we could claim the title of an international series before competitors even got a passport. Going to Montreal wasn't a distraction; it was a flanking maneuver.

We simultaneously recruited a volunteer army of friends and family ambassadors to run the ground game: Selica in Montreal, Joe's friend Anne in New York, another in Texas, and my sister AJ in Malibu. None of them had ever produced a race. We were teaching a raider force how to build a battlefield from scratch.

THE NAVIGATOR'S LOGIC

In the early stages of a movement, you cannot afford the establishment approach to marketing. You don't buy billboards; you buy the crowd. If you don't have a crowd, you must engineer the appearance of one. Lack of social proof is lethal because people are naturally risk-averse. By using the suggestion script and the fake photoshoot, we bypassed the hesitation and created social gravity.

Use aggressive, non-standard tactics to force-multiply your presence. Matt and Ben infiltrating campuses wasn't about theft; it was about bypassing the ad blockers of the modern mind. As Joe's reaction to the leftover cash proved, saving money can be a failure of vision. When you are in a land-grab phase, the goal is to overwhelm the objective, not to balance the ledger.

THE MARKET MIRROR: RED BULL

Red Bull didn't build their brand through Super Bowl ads; they built it through student brand managers. They put cars with giant cans on college campuses and infiltrated the nightlife. They manufactured social gravity by ensuring that the coolest person in the room was the one holding the product. They didn't buy the audience; they owned the environment. They turned their customers into a raider force that made the brand feel ubiquitous and inevitable before the traditional beverage giants even saw them coming.

MONDAY MORNING PROTOCOLS

1. The Social Gravity Hack: Identify where your target audience lives digitally or physically. Instead of buying a broad ad, deploy a high-touch raider like an intern or ambassador to infiltrate that space with a high-value, low-cost hook.
2. The Fabricated Reality Check: If your product is new, you lack social proof. Use tight-angle storytelling, focus on the intensity of the few to create the appearance of a movement for the many. Don't wait for the stadium to be full; make the front row look like a riot.

The Dorm Room Raiders had manufactured the gravity we needed. Through sheer hustle, we tilted the deck in our direction. We had the digital crowd, the fake photos had created real anticipation, and the mythology was starting to pulse in the CrossFit boxes. But social proof is a promissory note that eventually comes due. You can only fake the race until the first athlete steps up to the starting line.

On May 22, 2010, the spark finally hit the dirt at Catamount Ski Area. This wasn't a photoshoot or a Facebook script anymore, it was five hundred people expecting a transformation. As the first obstacles were set into place and the registration lines swelled, the chaos of reality collided with our prototype. We were about to find out who would melt and who would remain.

It was time for the first starting cannon. It was time to meet the Smoldering Man.

CHAPTER 10: THE SMOLDERING MAN

Transitioning from Theory to Operational Truth

Strategy is a hypothesis until it hits the dirt. This chapter is about the transition from fabricated reality to operational truth, the moment where your prototype meets the first five hundred customers and the chaos of the real world begins to provide the only data that matters.

THE BIRTH

Catamount Family Center, Williston, VT | May 22, 2010 |
Morning of the First Race

The venue was startlingly fresh, the kind of atmosphere you
only find in upstate Vermont on a late spring morning. The sun
was out, the grass was an aggressive, vibrant green, and the
birds were chirping with a rhythm that felt entirely too peaceful
for the violence we were about to unleash. There was a
distinct lack of corporate polish. As I walked the course for a
final check, I passed a pine tree. Underneath it was a sleeping
bag. One of our lead builders crawled out from the needles,
stood up, shook the debris off his jeans, and lit a cigarette.
That was our operations team. The air smelled of woodsmoke
and tilled earth. We had hired a local blacksmith to forge
medals on-site. The loud clang-clang of his hammer on the
iron anvil drifted across the empty field. It felt less like a
sporting event and more like a medieval siege camp.

THE GPS PANIC AND THE INVENTION OF HEATS

At 10:30 a.m. the day before the race, the math failed.
"Richard, the course is too short!" I had just finished my final
GPS pass. We had sold the racers a three-mile challenge, but
my screen showed a measly one and a half miles. I panicked.
Adding more trails meant sending racers on a long, boring run
without obstacles, violating the Spartan Ratio of effort versus
intensity.

We were short on resources once again. The obstacles were
in place so we couldn't move them. I came up with the Two-
Bike solution; pivot to two laps. We instantly doubled our
obstacles, but the solution created an immediate logistical
crisis. We couldn't start five hundred people at once on a two-
lap course without a bottleneck catastrophe. To solve the

math, we decided to release the racers in small waves of one hundred, every fifteen minutes. What was born of a GPS error became the industry standard. The heat system wasn't a strategic masterstroke; it was a survival tactic.

THE WAIVER CRISIS AND THE PARKING PROXY

At 8:00 a.m. on race morning, the mob began to form. Ben, our intern-turned-logistics-chief, was missing with the printed waivers. Ben had graduated from college the afternoon before, celebrated into the night, and was nowhere to be found. The line started to boil over. We looked amateur. I told Selica to start a virtual line, taking names on a clipboard to lower the temperature.

Joe rolled in, and I thought he would be as upset at the line as I was. To my surprise, he loved it. It makes the event look big, he said, beaming. When Ben finally arrived, I didn't hug him. I grabbed the waivers and yelled, "Go park cars!" This led to the kidnapping of Dan Luzzi. Dan had approached Joe in the chaos to get a school internship paper signed. Joe looked at him and said, "If I sign it, you are mine. Go to the parking lot. Don't let the cars sink." If you want to find out who belongs in your phalanx, put them in charge of five hundred cars sinking into a muddy Vermont field with zero instruction. Dan didn't quit; that morning forged a decade-long career.

THE ARROW FAILS TO LIGHT

The start line was finally set. We had built a straw man target for the opening ceremony. The plan was cinematic: an archer would fire a flaming arrow into the chest of the effigy, igniting a massive bonfire to signal the start of the Spartan era. The archer drew back. The crowd held its breath. Thwip. Perfect shot. Dead center in the chest. But physics intervened. The straw was too packed. The arrow's flame buried itself deep inside the torso and extinguished instantly. Instead of a roaring inferno, we got a sad wisp of gray smoke. The crowd stood in awkward silence. Richard didn't hesitate. He ran out with a red gas can, doused the hero, and lit it with a Bic lighter. Whoosh. The crowd cheered. When the fancy plan fails, grab the gas can.

THE GLADIATOR IN THE GLEN

Richard had purchased two six-foot pugil sticks—padded batons—for jousting in the festival area. But I decided to give one to a model we hired and hide him in the trees. We stationed Anthony, a man built like an oak tree, in a hidden glen in the pine forest. Whenever a racer came near him, wham! Anthony's pugil stick came down hard, making a dull thump against the racer's chest. We weren't trying to injure people, but a solid hit could send you flying back into the pines. As the day wore on, spectators began abandoning the festival area to walk into the woods. They wanted to see the carnage. It became a voyeuristic sport; the crowd cheered like it was the Roman Colosseum every time Anthony connected. I made the decision right there that the gladiator would move to the finish next time for all to see.

THE FESTIVAL FREAK SHOW

Back at the base, the vibe was medieval Woodstock. We had an archery range, an iron smith, and a fire twirler, a Vermont mountain hippie straight out of the '70s. She started her performance in a trance and stumbled, and a piece of burning moss detached from her baton, flying high into the crowd. I bolted from the finish line, terrified of a lawsuit for negligent burning by a hippie. The crowd dodged, and the twirler just fell on her rear end, laughing. I told Richard to shut her down immediately.

Onstage, our live music acts were met with mixed reviews. The first band was terrible, and the second picked the mood up some, but live music comes with large breaks in the show. The festival would grind from a party to a full halt each time a song ended.

THE SMOLDERING MAN

Despite the waivers, the arrow, and the hippie, the energy at the finish line was electric. Near the end of the day, I saw a man crossing the line who perfectly encapsulated the friction advantage. He had jumped over the fire pit, and his shirt was literally smoldering. He was covered in Vermont clay, bleeding from a scratch on his arm, and grinning like he'd just won the lottery. He didn't ask about his time. He just looked at me and said, "When is the next one?"

THE NAVIGATOR'S LOGIC

The first Spartan Race was a beautiful, smoking wreck. By every traditional business metric, it was a series of near catastrophes, but none of those consequences mattered. In the boardroom, we obsess over making the user experience as frictionless as possible. At Catamount, we learned that the right kind of friction actually creates a deeper connection. The racers didn't care that the waivers were late; they cared that they had discovered something deep about themselves in the mud.

Apply the gas can protocol: when your archer fails, don't wait for a new arrow. Use the resources you have to achieve the result. The crowd rewards the outcome, not the process.

Understand the voyeurism of struggle. People don't just want to suffer; they want to be seen suffering. Moving the gladiator to the finish line became our signature because it gave spectators a front-row seat to the spectacle. We weren't just building a race; we were armor-plating the human psyche. The smoldering man didn't want a refund for the long lines; he wanted to know where he could find that feeling again.

THE MARKET MIRROR: THE PEAK-END RULE

Psychologist Daniel Kahneman discovered that humans don't remember an entire experience; they remember the peak, the most intense part, and the end. Spartan mastered this by placing the gladiator in the woods and the fire jump. Even if the registration line was a disaster, the peak and the end were so intense that they created a systemic reboot. Most businesses try to make every touchpoint a level five. Spartan makes the beginning and middle a struggle, so the peak and the end feel like a level ten.

MONDAY MORNING PROTOCOLS

1. Identify the Smoldering Man Moment: Map your customer's journey. Where is the visceral point of transformation? If you don't have one, you are just providing a service. You need to engineer a moment that forces your customer to discover something new about themselves.
2. The Gas Can Pivot: Look at your most cinematic project—the one that relies on perfect timing, high-end tech, or a specific expert to succeed. Now, assume that archer fails. Write down your Gas Can Solution: the raw, unrefined, and manual method you will use to hit the deadline anyway. If you don't have a messy backup that works, your plan isn't a strategy; it's a hope.

The Smoldering Man had survived. We had emerged from the fire of the first race in Williston with more than just a proof of concept; we had identified the indestructible core of our team. We knew we could handle the chaos of a five-hundred-person starting line. But as the adrenaline of the first victory began to settle, a new kind of friction emerged: the temptation to stay safe.

It would have been easy to stay in Vermont and perfect the model in our own backyard. But in the world of operational piracy, safety is a slow death. While our competitors were still trying to figure out how to build a wooden wall, we decided to do something that defied conventional business logic for a three-month-old company. We didn't just want to expand; we wanted to invade. It was time to take the Spartan phalanx where the establishment couldn't easily follow. We were heading to Montreal. It was time for the border crossing.

CHAPTER 11: THE BORDER CROSSING

Flat-Packing Complexity for Global Scale

Every high-growth company eventually hits a border: a geographic, legal, or bureaucratic barrier that threatens to halt its momentum. Success in new markets requires flat-packing your complexity and deconstructing your product into its most modular, least threatening components.

THE SMUGGLERS

US-Canada Border | June 2010 | Status: The Border Crossing

"Now, tell me again. . . what are you guys doing?"

The Canadian officer's voice was thick with skepticism. He was circling our flatbed trailer like it was a crime scene. To be fair, it looked like one. The bed was a heap of scrap wood, brown cardboard boxes sealed with duct tape, coils of rusty barbed wire, and a bundle of garden shovel handles with nails glued into the ends. In the passenger seat sat Matt, clutching his passport. Beside him was the driver, Charlie, a retired logger in his mid-sixties. This was the moment the second-ever Spartan Race might fail before it even started. They had the entire race on the back of their trailer.

Matt stuck to the script: "We are staging a charity event in Quebec." The officers didn't look convinced. They poked at the spears and the shovel handles. They saw weapons; we saw obstacles. After agonizing minutes, the verdict was in: $400. The culprit wasn't the spears or the wire. It was the T-shirts. Because the shirts originated in China, they triggered a specific textile tariff. We paid the cash. The gates opened. The Hillbilly Convoy rolled into Canada. We had cleared the first obstacle, but we were about to hit the second.

THE IKEA NIGHTMARE

The crisis had actually begun back in Pittsfield. Dana, our primary builder, was a savant with wood. He knew exactly how every wall and ramp fit together. The problem? He didn't own a passport. We were forced to leave the brain in Vermont and send the hands—Jake, an intern—to Montreal. We had spent forty-eight hours dicing every piece of raw timber into pre-measured lengths and loading them like a giant game of Tetris. Jake assured us he knew the plan. He didn't.

Standing in the Montreal woods, looking at a pile of lumber, the realization hit: tribal knowledge had stayed in Vermont. Jake couldn't tell which beam went to which wall. This was catastrophic. We spent forty-eight hours reverse-engineering our own designs, guessing at bolt holes and tensioning straps by feel. It was *operational jazz*, making it up as we went along. The lesson learned here was that if your business relies on one guy named Dana, you don't have a business; you have a hobby. You need a *universal adapter*: a set of instructions so clear that a stranger can build the empire.

THE MONTREAL SWEATBOX

The ground crew: Richard, Selica, Matt, Ben, and Dan, were living the brand. They were crammed into a five-hundred-square-foot apartment in the city. One bedroom. One bathroom. A heatwave with no AC. The apartment smelled of dirty laundry and unwashed bodies. It was the kind of shared suffering that either breaks a team or bonds them for life. This was the phalanx forming in real-time.

Marketing in Montreal was another beast. In 2010, Canada was still Blackberry country. While the iPhone was gaining ground in the US, Blackberry held nearly 40 percent of the Canadian market. This added a layer of hardware friction to our Facebook hack, the JavaScript code didn't run smoothly on the Blackberry browser. The bigger friction was language. The pitch turned into a game of charades, pantomiming race, mud, and charity. But we found an international equalizer: alcohol. Matt and the team found that after three drinks, people were incredibly willing to hand over their phones to the crazy Americans. The script ran. The friend requests went out. We built a database of five hundred racers from zero, one beer at a time.

THE GLADIATOR PIVOT

In Williston, the gladiator was a hidden surprise in the woods. In Montreal, I made a strategic shift: the finish line gauntlet. We surrounded the finish line with hay bales and stationed the gladiator right before the timing mat. It transformed the race. Instead of a solitary struggle in the woods, the beat down became a spectator sport. We realized then that spectator value was a product we could sell. We weren't just creating a race for the athlete; we were creating a show for their friends.

THE LICENSING BATTLE

As the mud dried, Richard and Selica dropped a bomb: they were moving back to the UK. My first instinct was to see a system failure, but I recalibrated. This wasn't a loss; it was cell division. However, Joe wanted to own the international markets outright. "If we own it, we control it," Joe argued. He saw licensing as a leak in the hull; I saw it as the only way to keep the ship from sinking. I had to be the navigator of reality. We didn't have the capital to navigate Canadian labor laws or UK taxes.

I brought up the Ironman model. They licensed the brand to local experts who took the initial risk. Once the cash flow was stable, Ironman moved in and acquired them. I walked Joe through the logic of the leverage ratio. On one hand, ownership was a high-friction path where every dollar spent abroad was essentially robbed from the US front line. On the other hand, licensing was a low-friction strategy that allowed us to export the risk. Licensees provided the cash and the local knowledge, while we collected the royalties and protected the brand standards.

Joe's fire provided the ambition to go global, but the licensing model provided the rails. I drafted agreements for Richard and

Selica, and they signed them before leaving for the UK. This model eventually allowed Spartan to expand into forty countries.

THE NAVIGATOR'S LOGIC

Tribal knowledge is a scaling friction. To achieve global velocity, you must move from operational jazz (making it up as you go along) to a universal adapter system (a clear, repeatable system). The drag of tribal knowledge occurs when the how-to lives only inside the heads of a few key players, creating significant key-man risk. If those individuals leave, the system flat lines. When you face the staffing cliff of key personnel exiting, you must evolve the model so the hands don't matter. Otherwise you have a hobby and not a business.

The spark of expansion comes from cell division—the willingness to trade 100 percent control for 1,000 percent speed. Licensing allows you to use other people's money and local expertise to build your empire without draining your central resources.

THE MARKET MIRROR: MCDONALD'S

Ray Kroc didn't just sell hamburgers; he sold a universal adapter. He took the Speedee Service System and flat-packed it so that a teenager in Des Moines could produce the exact same result as the founders in California. By removing tribal knowledge, he enabled global velocity. He proved that the most complex systems are the ones that are the easiest to reproduce.

MONDAY MORNING PROTOCOLS

1. The Dana Audit: Identify the Dana in your office, the person whose head contains all the vital tribal

knowledge. If they weren't there tomorrow, would the system flat line? Begin flat-packing their logic into modular SOPs (standard operating procedures) immediately.

2. The Ownership vs. Velocity Calc: Are you trying to own 100 percent of a slow launch? Consider the licensing/franchise model. Trade total control for 1,000 percent speed. Use other people's money and local expertise to plant your flag in new territories.

The border crossing into Montreal proved that the Spartan virus could cross cultural lines. But as we turned our sights back to the US heartland, we realized that geographical scale requires a new kind of biological resilience. You can't conquer a continent quickly with an office of managers. To survive the brutal logistics of Year One, we needed a unit that could move, adapt, and repair itself in real-time. It was time to forge the nomadic phalanx.

CHAPTER 12: THE NOMADIC PHALANX

Eliminating Silos to Survive the Hyper-Growth Window

A single point of failure is a corporate death sentence disguised as specialization. In the volatile first year of hyper-growth, you cannot afford departments or titles that act as silos. You need a *nomadic phalanx*: a high-mobility team where every member understands the adjacent role well enough to step in when the pressure hits.

The neighborhood was a graveyard of industrial ambition. Ben Killary stood in front of a massive, salt-stained brick building that looked like it hadn't seen a human being since the Industrial Revolution. Ben fumbled with a heavy set of keys, the lock groaning, a metallic scream echoing through the empty street, and then the door gave way.

Inside, the air was thick with wet concrete and ancient dust. The floor was a debris field of shattered glass and rusted pipes. There was no electricity, no heat, and no running water. This was the command center for our expansion. Joe had purchased this condemned barbershop years ago and told Ben: "Why pay for a hotel when you have a perfectly good concrete floor?" Ben pitched a $40 Walmart tent in the middle of the room to keep the rats out. As he zipped himself in, a siren wailed in the distance, the soundtrack of a city that rarely welcomes the unprepared.

THE PAPER CREDIT CARD

To fund the street operation in NYC, Ben carried a corporate card. It wasn't plastic. It was a grainy photocopy of Joe's driver's license and AmEx, folded and unfolded so many times it was as soft as fabric. Ben would walk into bars to buy rounds for potential customers, hand the bartender this piece of paper, and pray. Most laughed. Some called the cops. It was humiliating, scrappy, and effective. Our local ambassador, Anne, eventually rescued Ben from the boarded-up building, and Dan Luzzi joined them in her home for the New York blitz. They dressed like gladiators on Wall Street by day and hit Sean McGuire's bar by night. We ended up with our first one-thousand-person event just two and a half months after Vermont.

THE WALL OF VALOR

Floyd Bennett Air Field, Brooklyn, NY | August 2010 | Status: The Brand Soul

We were done with the scrap wood phase; we were building a mobile arsenal. This event marked the entrance of Russell Cohen, who became the lead builder for Spartan for the next ten years. His work ethic was unparalleled. Before every first heat, we'd look at one another and say sarcastically, "What could go wrong?" Russell was the start of us building redundancy on the Operations Team.

Our New York gladiator experience was next level. We hired three gladiators and boxed the arena in with metal bicycle fencing so there was no escape. As we built out the course on the abandoned airfield tarmac, Russell constructed an extra eight-foot wall we didn't need. "Let's leave it in the festival area," he said. "Give people markers." We expected graffiti; what we got was a sanctuary. People wrote about the stage 4 cancer they were fighting and the one hundred pounds they had lost and scribbled messages to fathers who had passed away. We realized this wall wasn't just lumber; it was the brand soul. We told the racers, "This wall travels with us." It became a piece of meaningful friction, connecting the grief of a New Yorker to the triumph of a Texan.

THE WAR WITH NATURE

Amesbury, MA | August 2010 | Status: Biological Attack

I stood on top of the hill at the Amesbury sports complex, admiring over 1,200 racers stretched across the course. Then I saw her: a very pregnant and incredibly fit woman heading toward the gladiators at the finish. I bolted. "Pregnant lady! No one touches her!" She passed unharmed, likely giving birth to the first Spartan baby soon after.

But the real threat was hidden. A massive mud wasp nest had been disturbed by the vibration of a thousand runners. They were pissed. To make matters worse, the course was accidentally threaded through poison ivy. We rerouted mid-race, but Nature had already cast its vote. The aftermath was expensive; racers tracked five tons of swamp mud into the carpeted complex and abandoned piles of ruined clothes in the locker rooms. We had to hire a hazmat-style crew just to get invited back the following year.

The largest impact of this race was the contribution of Mike Morris. Mike still owned two fitness studios in Massachusetts and was only involved in this one event in the first year. But it was clear that scaling was going to require more people I could trust to plan and execute races.

TEXAS: PIGS, SNAKES, AND DRUNK BUILDERS

Burnet, Texas | October 2010 | Status: The Wild West

Texas was our first cold launch. I saw feral pigs darting through the scrub brush and learned about snake circles—thirty-foot rings of bare sand around water that snakes won't cross for fear of hawks. Russell had hired a local builder (also named Russell) who showed up every morning with a thirty-pack of Busch Light. He drank steadily from dawn to dusk, yet his lines were perfectly straight and his work ethic was unbreakable. We only had seven hundred racers, which felt like a setback. We also fought the venue owner over a $1,500 bill for a stage he built that essentially became his new patio. We settled up, knowing we needed larger venues and better local partners.

We tried to create redundancy on-the-cheap in Texas with the second local carpenter. But it backfired. Any lessons learned during that cycle would only travel forward with Russell. We need to create a consistent crew in order to scale.

Navigator's Note: In attendance at the first race in Texas, was a gentleman by the name of Yancy Culp. He would go on to participate in many future Spartan events, including the Death Race, and eventually join the company. More on that later.

MALIBU: THE MACHETE AND THE DISTRACTION

Calamigos Ranch, Malibu, CA | December 2010 | Status: Operational Friction

Malibu was the final 2010 test. I spent the week hacking through forty feet of dense brush with a machete to create a bush tunnel, dodging Pacific rattlesnakes the whole way. The property was beautiful but had no on-site parking, requiring a massive shuttle bus operation from the PCH. Back at the hotel, we were running a bag-packing assembly line, stuffing 1,500 race packets by hand. In the middle of this grueling work, Joe walked in with adult film star Savanna Samson to promote a recovery device called the Body Wrench. Savanna proceeded to lie on the floor in the middle of our assembly line to demonstrate the device.

Productivity hit zero. Matt, Ben, and Dan stopped working. Jaws hit the floor. It was the ultimate clash of cultures: the grunts trying to execute a race vs. the ringmaster trying to sell a story. Joe named her "Spartan of the Week" and created a racy Facebook ad. It caused massive internal friction; none of us believed she represented the brand, but Joe was just hunting for eyeballs.

THE SUV RESCUE

Late in the afternoon, the shuttle bus drivers timed out and left hundreds of racers stranded in the canyon. Frustration was turning to riot. Back at the festival, our bag check had devolved into a giant, disorganized pile of gear. As the sun set and the line grew, we offered free beer to anyone who would abandon their place in line. I jumped into a rented SUV and drove to the front of the angry mob. "Who is a DRIVER?" I yelled. I drove the drivers down to their cars so they could rescue their carpools. I turned the twenty-minute ride into a focus group, de-escalating the situation while getting raw intel. By the time the racers reached their cars, they were calm. The rental company, however, was not happy about the mud on the leather seats.

This was a valuable lesson in redundancy in a crisis. The longer I was sucked into dealing with a single situation, the longer the rest of the event went on unsupervised. We needed more hands to manage the events as they grew and we needed people who could cross-train and be ready to jump into other roles at a moment's notice.

THE NAVIGATOR'S LOGIC

Scaling a global brand requires a violent, constant tension between Logistics and The Circus. Logistics is the structural plumbing, the boring, essential math that ensures the shuttle buses show up and the timing chips work. The Circus is the raw, chaotic spectacle, the fire, the mud, and the emotional high that gives the brand its soul.

If you have too much Circus, the event collapses into an unmanageable mess. If you have too much Logistics, the brand becomes a sterile commodity and dies. The Spartan advantage is found in the friction between the two.

A tactical example of this tension was our decision to weaponize the Hero Shot—the high-impact, in-race photo of a racer conquering an obstacle. While our competitors followed the traditional logic of charging thirty dollars per image, we chose to give them away for free. By sacrificing immediate revenue, we turned every racer into a viral billboard. If you give people a premium tool to brag, they will do your marketing for you. It was a strategic move to trade short-term cash for long-term global velocity. The fast eat the slow.

Scaling also requires a Nomadic Phalanx: a culture where everyone is a high-level generalist. In the early days of a movement, specialized titles are a form of friction that prevents speed. The person who packs the heavy gear must also be able to drive the lead SUV or de-escalate a mob at the finish line. We didn't need "managers"; we needed teammates who could hold the line regardless of the terrain.

Ultimately, the Wall of Valor—the physical boundary where racers face their final test—proved our most enduring lesson: people don't want an easy experience; they want a sacred one. The suck isn't the problem you solve; it's the product you sell.

THE MARKET MIRROR: TOYOTA (THE ANDON CORD)

In a Toyota factory, any worker on the line can pull the *Andon cord* (a tool in manufacturing that allows workers to immediately signal a problem on the production line, temporarily stop production, and request assistance to resolve quality or safety issues) to stop the entire production if they see a defect. This requires every worker to understand the whole system, not just their silo. They are a phalanx, if the person to the left sees a failure, the whole wall reacts. By empowering the individual to stop the machine, Toyota ensures that quality is everyone's responsibility, effectively eliminating the single point of failure that plagues most manufacturing giants.

MONDAY MORNING PROTOCOLS

1. The No Silo Cross-Train: Pick two departments that rarely speak (e.g., Sales and Accounting). Swap one team member from each for forty-eight hours. This

eliminates the hero bottleneck, where only one person knows how to get the job done, and builds the role redundancy required for hyper-growth.
2. The Vanity Vector: Identify the "hero shot" in your business—the moment your customer feels like a champion. Stop trying to monetize that moment; give it away for free. Let your customers be your marketing department.

The nomadic phalanx had survived the first tour of duty. We had moved from a single muddy field in Vermont to five major cities in less than a year. We had proven the prototype, scaled the spark, and manufactured a social gravity that was starting to pull the entire fitness world into our orbit. But as we looked toward 2011, the pirate phase was ending. The market was no longer a series of small skirmishes; it was a full-scale war.

THE SPARK MANIFESTO: VELOCITY IS THE PRIMARY PROTECTION

You have exited the launch phase. You have seen how a few guys in a Hell's Kitchen basement weaponized social proof, faked the crowd until it was real, and began a series of brutal experiments with field penalties to handle the friction of the unknown. We hadn't yet standardized a universal currency for failure, which was still being forged in the heat of the first races, but the search for a definitive Law of the Land had begun.

As we moved from the basement to the mountains, we learned that in high-growth environments, **Velocity is your primary protection.** You don't solve friction by stopping; you solve it by accelerating through the heat until the structure hardens.

To transition from a startup to a superpower, you must carry the Four Laws of the Spark with you:

1. OODA Loop Superiority: You win not by having the better plane, but by processing reality faster than the competition. You prioritize integrated velocity over the fortress of safety.
2. The Forgiveness Protocol: You stop waiting for the permit. You launch imperfectly, deploy the sacrificial lamb (the Binns maneuver) to absorb the heat, and let the market dictate the final design.
3. The Vanity Vector: You recognize that Identity is more profitable than utility. You give away the hero shot for free, knowing that your customers' desire to brag is your most powerful unpaid marketing engine.
4. Standardized Pain: You remove the operational jazz and replace it with a universal adapter. You turn

heroics into algorithms, ensuring that the brand can scale without requiring the founder to be in the mud.

By the end of 2010, the nomadic phalanx had survived the Year of the Firsts. We had taken a $100,000 napkin and turned it into an international series. We used Two-Bike Math to stretch our meager resources, outlasted the Sleep Monster in the trenches, and identified the Smoldering Men who wouldn't break. The spark had caught. We weren't just a startup anymore; we were a phenomenon.

But success is its own kind of friction. The brushfire was out of control, threatening to outrun our ability to contain it. You now have the viral momentum, the international footprint, and the phalanx unit required to execute under fire. However, individual heroics and dorm room raider energy can only ignite a brand; they cannot sustain a global empire.

As we scale, the friction of the world changes. You are no longer fighting for a few hundred likes; you are fighting for multi-million dollar sponsorships and global dominance. To survive the next phase, we have to stop being a traveling circus and start being a superpower. We are moving from the sweatbox to the C-suite.

Welcome to Part III.

Part III: THE SUPERPOWER
(Hyper-Growth Tactics)

By the dawn of 2011, the spark that had ignited in a Vermont hay field had become a sprawling, untamed wildfire. We had graduated from being a scrappy, under-the-radar startup and were now a high-velocity market disruptor. But as any operational architect will tell you, the more rapidly you expand your footprint, the more dangerously thin your logistical infrastructure becomes.

THE SIXTEEN-POINT EXPANSION

2011 | Continental US

We had successfully moved beyond managing a single, localized race to a global growth strategy that felt less like a business rollout and more like managing sixteen concurrent launches. The map was aggressive: up and down the East Coast, pushing into the Midwest through Illinois, scaling the Rockies in Denver, and establishing roots in the canyons of California. Since we only had one event in January and one in

December, the other fourteen were compressed into a ten-month sprint.

This created a treadmill that never stopped. I would be standing on a ranch in Texas, marking the course, while taking a call from a venue owner in Illinois about a race three months away. At night, instead of sleeping, I was in the hotel lobby, trying to clear an inbox that refilled faster than I could type. This was permanent operational redlining. A seven-day work week, twelve to fifteen hours a day of physical labor, in whatever weather the gods threw at us. The fatigue became a critical system risk. This is the type of sprint you need to dedicate yourself to if you plan a new business. It is not for the faint of heart.

THE SCRAP HEAP: PROTOTYPING THE FAIL

When you redline the engine, things break. I don't want you to think that everything we did was successful. In the name of speed, we had several spectacular failures that served as our most expensive special tests.

Joe hired a group to improve our efficiency when we loaded and unloaded the trailers. They cut a massive side door into the trailer so we could load from the side and back simultaneously. It seemed like a good idea, but the structural integrity failed during a long-distance haul. The trailer snapped in half on the side of the highway. We had to buy another trailer and send it and a crew out to salvage the contents from the side of the road. Lesson: You cannot optimize a system if you compromise the foundation.

In Virginia, Nick Moore had found a paintball facility to host our event. We experimented with a paintball machine gun as an obstacle. As you crawled through a tarp tunnel, you would be peppered with high-velocity paintballs. I took my kids to the beta test, and the feedback was visceral: it hurt, it was arbitrary, and everyone hated it. We learned that suck must have a purpose; if it's just abuse, it's not a Spartan obstacle.

Even our gladiators, once the signature of the finish line, became a friction bottleneck. Elite racers found them unfair. We couldn't have prize money at stake when the gladiators could choose whom to attack. But it was the safety of the gladiators themselves that turned out to be the issue. Racers started to organize groups that would assemble just before the gladiators and attack them out of pure, adrenaline-fueled aggression. We had to remove them to protect the integrity and the safety of the finish.

The fatigue tax was real. At Mountain Creek, a ski hill in New Jersey, an exhausted crew member dozed off for a split second, crashing a truck into a main water pipe. We had ATVs flipping in ditches because the drivers were too drained to navigate the mud. We dug through another pipe in Utah with a backhoe. We were redlining the people as hard as the machines.

THE REGISTRATION RIFT: ASSET VS. ARBITRAGE

In 2011, I made a strategic move to secure our technical independence. I brought in a colleague from Bristol Technology to build our own proprietary registration system. At the time, we were using a site that was designed for runners, and it didn't have everything we needed to manage an obstacle race. The logic was bulletproof: we wouldn't be at the mercy of a third-party roadmap, and by charging a small platform fee, the system would fund its own development. It turned a cost center into a revenue-generating asset.

I was building a foundation. Joe was looking at the speedometer. By 2012, the business was starved for cash.

Joe's obsession with growth and Facebook spending had created a cash burn rate that our current revenue couldn't sustain. While I was on vacation in Utah, my one moment of offline time, the Fire-Breather made an executive decision. He cut a deal with Active.com. He didn't call to consult; he called to inform. Active was going to front us cash against future ticket sales and provide a massive marketing megaphone. Joe saw a lifeline; I saw us mortgaging our sovereignty for a short-term cash injection.

THE CASH FLOW TRAP: BUYING FOLLOWERS WITH PAYROLL

This era introduced us to the dangerous trick model of event cash flow. In the event world, you collect money today for a product you don't have to deliver for six months. To a Fire-Breather, that cash balance looks like fuel sitting in a tank. Joe was unstoppable on Facebook. He realized early that he could buy a community. He would snatch up every cent of revenue we generated and pour it into ads to buy more followers and more heat. Joe was implementing an aggressive blitzscaling spend while simultaneously demanding that we become profitable. We were living on the edge of bankruptcy every single month to fund the top of the funnel.

THE BIRTH OF THE BURPEE

The 30-burpee penalty is now a global Spartan standard, but it was born out of a logistical failure. We noticed that obstacles like the monkey bars and the spear throw were causing massive bottlenecks. Early on, if you failed an obstacle, you had to go back and retry. But the retries were clogging the flow. We needed a penalty that was space-efficient, required no equipment, and was hard enough to deter skipping. We had experimented with different exercises and penalty loops, but it was hard to manage. We needed to standardize, and the burpee was the answer. We treated the office like a lab. We had Matt, Ben, and Dan drop and do burpees while we timed them. Ten reps were too fast. Twenty reps were getting there. Thirty reps? That was the breaking point. It spiked the heart rate just enough to equal the effort of the obstacle.

As we launched The Beast at Killington, our answer to the thirteen-mile endurance model, the math of our penalties started to break. If a racer failed six obstacles, they faced 180 burpees. That isn't a penalty; it's a funeral. This led to our first major segmentation strategy, where we created a three-tiered system within the product: Elites, Age Groupers, and Open racers. We had absolute enforcement for the Elites, where integrity is the product; strict standards for the Competitive heat; and an honor system for the Open heat that allowed people to self-select their suffering.

Welcome to the whirlwind that was our hyper-growth years. In fact, it wasn't just a whirlwind; it was a full-blown hurricane.

CHAPTER 13: THE HURRICANE

The Physics of Territory and the Cost of Geographical Dominance

Expansion is a force multiplier for both your strengths and your hidden weaknesses.

THE HURRICANE PIVOT (THE GO/NO-GO)

Amesbury, Massachusetts | August 2011 | Status: State of Emergency

The radar on the laptop screen was a swirl of angry reds and purples. Hurricane Irene wasn't just a storm; it was a wall of water aimed directly at New England. Mike Morris and I were on a conference call, looking at the projections. "We have to pull the plug," I said. The risk wasn't just the race; it was the roads, the bridges, and the emergency services. We got Joe on the line. He scoffed. "We aren't canceling," he said. "Spartans don't cancel because of rain."

"Joe, this isn't rain," Mike countered. "The governor is declaring a State of Emergency." The local Emergency Management Agency made the final call: the event was shut down. No permits. No exceptions. Mike and I breathed a sigh of relief, thinking the friction had ended. We were wrong. Joe pivoted instantly. "Fine, the event is canceled," he said. "But I'm putting out a blast on Facebook: anyone who wants to work out in the eye of the storm, meet me at 5:00 a.m."

At 5:00 a.m., in 50 mph winds and torrential rain, fifty people showed up. Joe led them through the storm. They carried sandbags up the mountain and did burpees in the mud. They loved it. We had accidentally invented a new product: the Hurricane Heat. It wasn't a race; it was a team-based suffer-fest led by the founders. It continues to be a core offering for those seeking the next level of challenge. If the bridge is washed out, you swim. As a side note, Hurricane Irene lives on in our lexicon; today, if a major weather event like lightning requires the team to clear a course, it goes out over our networks as "Code Irene."

GLOBAL INFILTRATION

If 2010 was a pilot program, 2011 was the year we unleashed a global juggernaut. We nearly tripled our footprint, managing sixteen events in the US while pushing into the UK and Canada. We were flying the plane while adding two engines in mid-air. To survive, we shifted our strategy: geography became our moat. We moved from flat fairgrounds to the hardest ski mountains we could find. Difficult terrain separates the fun runs from the sport. But as we pushed into the wild, the wild began to push back.

You cannot scale a movement if the founder is the only one who knows where the gas can is hidden. To manage a sixteen-point expansion, we built a decentralized network. I brought on Nick Moore and Mike Morris as our primary race directors. I split the map, giving each a territory and a mandate to execute the Spartan standard with total autonomy. To grow, I had to be comfortable with delegating the very role I was brought on to do. But I trusted Mike & Nick. We also recruited Addy Goodvibes and Harold Zundel, both from the adventure racing world. This was a deliberate system requirement. When a truck gets stuck at 4:00 a.m. on a mountain in Vermont, a professional looks for the handbook; an adventure racer looks for a winch and a coffee.

THE DRILL FROM HELL

Temecula, California | January 2011 | Build Cycle

"I'm not in control!" Nick Moore's voice was unusually panicked. The box truck we were in was sliding uncontrollably down the thin, muddy spine of the Temecula hills. The weather had turned from sunny to a cold front that brought snow flurries and then rain, turning the fire roads into grease. We had just delivered the bones of a cargo net to the peak and were headed back down to base camp. The yellow rental truck slid precariously, with drop-offs on both sides, and for a moment I was certain we were about to slide over the edge. We finally hit a flatter section, and the truck came to a halt. My heart was racing. We were safe, but stuck. We spent the next hour wedging boards under the wheels to get out of the mud.

Back on the flatland, Russell Cohen had an idea for a new obstacle: the Hercules Hoist. The design included a heavy weight attached to thick rope and wrapped around a pulley. The competitors would have to pull hand over hand to lift the weight up to over 20 feet in the air. It would require a high beam to suspend the pulleys.

Today, we use heavy equipment like telehandlers to set these up. In 2011, we had three old telephone poles, a hand-held ground drill, and twenty national guardsmen. The drill was a beast, a gas-powered auger that kicked with bone-jarring force every time it hit a rock. It took over an hour to drill the two holes deep enough to hold the massive structure. As we lifted the 1,500-pound structure using nothing but ropes and grit, I stepped backward into an open post hole. Snap. I thought I had broken my leg. I spent the next few hours limping through the build, fueled by adrenaline and ibuprofen. But like the ancient Spartans, we pushed and pulled on the beast of an obstacle until it stood up tall, then slowly walked it until it dropped into the holes. In fact, we built it so well that we couldn't get it down. We left the poles standing, a modern ruin in the California desert that remained there for many years.

THE ARIZONA FIRESTORM

In Arizona, the pressure to out-spectacle ourselves nearly caused a catastrophe. Joe wanted a fire jump that looked epic, so we built it inside a concrete drainage ditch. We didn't realize the concrete would act as a kiln. When we lit the pile of wood, the heat reflected and intensified into a localized firestorm. To make matters worse, Nick had put the fire jump at the beginning of the race. The athletes would be jockeying for position, and the potential for someone to get bumped into the kiln was real. The gasoline-soaked wood shot flames that roared ten feet high just as the first wave of racers approached. "It's too hot!" I yelled. We jumped in with spear sticks, fighting the blaze to beat it down in time for the first rush of racers. A few racers did get singed. New SOP: "Racers must go through a water obstacle immediately before the fire." Safety rules were being written in real-time.

THE TEXAS DEAD FISH

By June, we were back in Texas at a new location with fewer pigs. The new venue had a large pond, so we created a bucket carry around the perimeter. Racers would fill their buckets with water from the pond, then circumnavigate the water and dump their buckets out. Thousands of feet churned the bank into a muddy mess. We saw a dead fish floating on the surface, then another, and another. By the end of the day, the surface was covered in dead fish. We had suffocated them with silt. It turned out the landowner had stocked that pond for fishing and was definitely not happy. Beyond the cost of restocking, we learned that scale has consequences. We were no longer just running through nature; we were impacting it. The bigger the events grew, the harder it was becoming to find locations that could handle the impact. We began implementing remediation plans to ensure we left every venue better than we found it.

CHRIS DAVIS: THE 700-POUND SPARTAN

At the 2011 Atlanta race, Chris Davis showed up weighing nearly seven hundred pounds. Most would have seen the obstacles as impossible; Chris saw them as necessary. Nearing the end of the day, the build crew is usually like a swarm of ants, dismantling obstacles the moment the last racer passes, but I radioed the team to hold the finish. I escorted Chris through the back half of the course. I felt that at any moment we would need to call the medical team in to help him. He wore a white T-shirt that had turned muddy brown from the swamp. He had to stop constantly to catch his breath, struggling up the muddy banks for what felt like an hour. But he refused to quit.

When he finally crawled through the last mud pit, we had the entire crew there to cheer him on. The festival was empty, but the staff and Joe were waiting. We cheered him across the line. Joe intervened on the spot. "If you're serious about your journey back to health, come to the farm," he told Chris. Chris moved to Vermont and lived by the code. Over the next eighteen months, he lost nearly four hundred pounds. He proved that Spartan wasn't just an event; it was an intervention. We proved that we were not just selling race tickets, we were selling a lifestyle.

THE MAFIA DUFFEL BAGS

In 2011, the world was still cash-heavy. We charged for parking, merchandise, and food, leaving us with staggering sums of small bills at the end of every weekend. We didn't want to pay for armored trucks back then; we had backpacks. I became the reluctant courier of the mafia bags, regular backpacks stuffed with tens of thousands of dollars in muddy, sweaty bills. There is a specific look a bank teller gives you when you slide a muddy backpack across the counter and start stacking piles of twenty-dollar bills. To them, we looked like drug dealers. To us, we were just trying to clear the books so we could fly to the next city. Scale increases risk. Statistics were catching up to us. We were no longer a backyard club; we were an industry.

THE NAVIGATOR'S LOGIC

Growth is not a linear path; it is a series of thermal runaways. When a hurricane shuts down your primary product, the superpower logic creates a new high-intensity offering out of the eye of the storm. You must learn to view terrain as a moat. If you expand onto flat ground, you are a commodity. By hunting for the hardest ski mountains, you create a geographical moat that competitors cannot easily replicate. You move from the fun run to the sport.

Each new event caused us to evolve. Sometimes we planned those evolutions, other times the events, the participants, the weather, the terrain or the market forced us to evolve. You must be committed to your core principles yet adaptable at the same time.

As you grow, you must own the total consequences of your scale, from environmental impacts like the silt in Texas to the logistical friction of cash management. Your product isn't the race; it's the transformation. Scaling the stories of racers like Chris Davis is more valuable to the brand's longevity than scaling the logistics. Your mission is to maintain these personal touches even as the volume of the business threatens to turn your customers into mere numbers.

THE MARKET MIRROR: PATAGONIA

As Patagonia scaled, they realized their environmental impact was their primary friction point. Their success was impacting the very wilderness they celebrated. Instead of ignoring the cost of their growth, they made remediation their brand moat; a competitive advantage not easily replicated. They famously launched the "Don't Buy This Jacket" campaign and invested heavily in sustainable supply chains. They realized that to maintain high-level influence, you must own the total consequences of your scale. You don't just sell a product; you manage the footprint it leaves behind.

MONDAY MORNING PROTOCOLS

1. The Structural Gap Audit: Identify one area of your business where you are moving forward without a safety net, a legal liability, a data security gap, or a broken process. Don't wait for the system to snap. Fill the hole today, even if it requires grit and ropes to bridge the gap temporarily.
2. The Hurricane Heat Pivot: Look at your biggest recent failure, such as a canceled project or a lost client. Don't just apologize. Ask what new product exists in the eye of this storm. How can you turn a "No-Go" into a high-intensity offering for your most loyal believers?
3. The Legacy Professionalization: Identify the one scrappy process you are still running that looks like an amateur operation to your partners. This is your scale drag. Set a deadline to automate or professionalize this process by the end of the month.

The 2011 expansion proved we could plant the flag. We had survived the hurricanes, the firestorms, and the backpacks of cash. We had successfully scaled the physics of the map, but as we looked at the competitors entering the space, we realized that geographical footprint wasn't enough. Warrior Dash was for the masses. Tough Mudder was for the teams. New entries were popping up daily, like Rugged Maniac and Savage Race. Even Don Mann was hired to run an obstacle start-up. We needed something that was for the individual soul, a distance so daunting it would act as a filtration system for the entire industry. It was time to return to the Green Mountains of Vermont to unleash the ultimate gatekeeper.

CHAPTER 14: THE BEAST

Building a Brand Moat through Extreme Difficulty

In a marketplace obsessed with reducing friction, the most powerful way to build a brand moat is to do the opposite: lean into the extreme. Most companies compete on convenience; elite brands compete on unique difficulty. By owning the hardest version of your product, you create an insurmountable barrier for competitors who are optimized for the middle of the road.

THE MOUNTAIN

Killington Ski Resort, Vermont | September 2011 | Status: The Beast

"Why is there a giant tire in the starting corral?" I stood at the base of the mountain, squinting against the early morning sun. Two guys stood next to a six-foot tractor tire, a four-hundred-pound doughnut of tread-worn rubber. It looked like it belonged on an earthmover, not a starting line. "What's going on?" I asked. They grinned, nervous. They were friends of Joe's. Their goal wasn't just to run the thirteen miles; it was to flip, roll, and drag that monster to the summit of the Beast of the East.

I looked up at the black diamond slope. It was vertical warfare. If they rolled it, gravity would turn it into a runaway steamroller that would crush anyone behind them. They would have to flip it. One. Rep. At. A. Time. I gave them the nod since they were not officially part of the event. As the gun went off, I watched them heave it over the first timing mat with a ground-shaking thud. Hours later, I heard the report: they had lost control on a downhill section. The tire careened into the forest, snapping trees like twigs. They had to drag it out of the underbrush like they were wrestling a bear. They finished in the dark long after the rest of the course was cleared. They weren't officially in the race, but that tire was a metaphor for our entire 2011 season: we were no longer just running; we were moving heavy weight uphill.

THE VERTICAL WAR (THE BRAND MOAT)

Killington changed the geometry of the sport. Until then, most obstacle races, including ours, were relatively flat. Killington was vertical warfare. I stood at the base and looked up the black diamond slope. It was carnage. The racers looked like a line of ants trying to summit an anthill. Zigzagging lines formed as people desperately tried to lessen the grade. Others just sat in the dirt, chests heaving, realizing they had started too fast.

The death march up was brutal, but the descent was worse. Descending a steep ski slope on exhausted legs destroys your quads. I watched racers crumble, their legs turning to jelly as they desperately tried to stop themselves from tumbling. We realized then that verticality was our moat. Anyone can dig a mud pit in a cow pasture. Very few can rent a mountain.

THE THREE-TIERED KINGDOM

In 2011 we were in an all-out war with Tough Mudder. We were gorilla marketing at their events and constantly battling for who had the hardest product. At the time, Tough Mudders were six to eight miles long. So we entered the 2011 season with a new product called the Super. Now we had a product equal to theirs, plus the benefit of the original three-mile product we now called the Sprint. But Tough Mudder upped the ante. They took their events up to thirteen miles. We responded with the event at Killington. In the winter, Killington marketed itself as The Beast of the East. That's how The Beast was born.

Killington was the moment our product tiering finally clicked. At first, we had a debate about simply renaming the Super to the Beast. But there were many people who liked the Super because it had more running. I saw that we were closely mimicking the running world which had 5Ks, 10Ks, and half marathons. To dominate the market, we needed a progression—a ladder of pain that kept people engaged for years, not just one weekend. We built a hierarchy of friction:

- The Sprint: (3–5 Miles). The Gateway Drug. Accessible, fast, punchy.

- The Super: (8–10 Miles). The Middle Ground. More obstacles, more technicality.
- The Beast: (13+ Miles). The Destination. Vertical punishment for the fanatic.

By creating the Beast, we weren't just adding a race; we were creating an ecosystem. And that ecosystem was starting to appeal to world-class athletes.

THE HUMAN MACHINE (HOBIE CALL)

The Beast attracted a new species: Hobie Call. Hobie was a runner with Olympic Trials marathon speed who saw in Spartan a sport that finally rewarded functional athleticism over pure track speed. Hobie was a machine. Compact, shirtless, with a power-to-weight ratio that defied physics. He didn't just run; he flowed. He would hit an eight-foot wall and vault it without breaking stride. His presence validated the idea that this wasn't just a challenge; it was a sport.

But Hobie didn't just participate; he monopolized the podium. He went on an absolute tear, winning dozens of races and building an undefeated streak that seemed mathematically impossible in an environment governed by mud and chaos. He was the first true student of the Spartan meta. While other strongmen and runners muscled their way through the course, burning massive amounts of energy fighting the terrain, Hobie engineered absolute efficiency.

He mathematically deconstructed the friction. He perfected the exact balance point of the spear throw. He figured out how to lock the heavy gravel bucket high on his chest to maintain his center of gravity. He realized that the fastest way through barbed wire wasn't to crawl, but to roll. He didn't fight the obstacles; he absorbed them. His dominance was so absolute that it handed us the ultimate PR weapon: the Bounty. We put a massive target on his back, publicly offering a cash prize that eventually scaled to $100,000 to anyone who could beat him. It was a masterclass in driving the market. By leveraging Hobie's invincibility, we baited the trap. It forced the world's elite triathletes, CrossFitters, and marathoners to look at our race and say, "I can beat that guy." When they showed up to try, they realized how brutal the Spartan ecosystem truly was. Most of them failed.

THE MARK OF THE BEAST (THE TATTOO)

I was observing the registration line where racers checked in when I saw a guy wearing a cutoff shirt. On his shoulder was a fresh, scabbing tattoo of the Spartan helmet. "Is that real?" I asked. He nodded. He wasn't the only one. We dragged Joe over to look. It was a shock to the system. I'd seen Harley-Davidson tattoos. I'd seen Apple stickers. But we were a startup. Why would someone permanently mark their body with our logo?

The answer wasn't about the race; it was about transformation. Most people live lives of quiet, climate-controlled comfort. Spartan was the first time they had been cold, wet, exhausted, and genuinely afraid, only to realize they could handle it. The tattoo wasn't a commercial. It was a certificate of rebirth. It was their way of saying: "I am no longer the person who sits on the couch. I am a person who finishes." We leaned into it. We brought tattoo artists on-site at future events. If you finished the Beast, you could get inked right there in the mud.

THE SKI RESORT STRATEGY

Killington taught us a hard lesson in inventory science and logistical science. In the past, we sold generic Spartan Tour shirts. Safe, reusable inventory. For Killington, we printed specific Killington Beast 2011 gear. The risk: if it rains, the shirts are worthless trash. The reality: scarcity drives demand. The specific gear sold out by noon. People didn't want a shirt; they wanted armor.

Killington solidified our operational strategy. We stopped looking for parks. We started looking for chairlifts. Ski resorts solved 50 percent of our headaches instantly: parking built for thousands, real toilets, food and beverage services and the vertical gain we needed to separate ourselves from the fun runs. We also learned some valuable lessons. The rugged terrain cut off our line of sight for our radio communications. We needed repeaters on the tops of the hills if we didn't want black-out zones. It also took longer to haul materials to the top of ski slopes. As we solved each new challenge, the payback was enormous. From that point on, the first search wasn't for fields—it was for mountains.

THE NAVIGATOR'S LOGIC

Operating on flat ground where the barrier to entry is minimal is a trap. If your business model is easy to replicate, you have no competitive moat. You win by owning the terrain that others find unreasonable. Intentionally seeking out the most challenging environments uses physical and logistical complexity to filter out low-commitment competitors. Leveraging an outlier like Hobie Call defines the upper limit of your product. Using elite performance attracts high-value, high-output participants who seek a definitive standard. Finally, if your product has no progression, it has no lifespan. You must move from a single one-size-fits-all offering to a hierarchy of intensity.

THE MARKET MIRROR: CROSSFIT

CrossFit didn't just sell workouts. They sold a structured progression that turned a gym routine into a multi-year career.

The CrossFit Open is an annual event accessible to everyone, acting as their Sprint equivalent. The Regionals are technical, demanding, and selective, mirroring our Super. The Games are elite, televised, and extreme, representing the Beast. By creating this hierarchy, they turned fitness into a lifecycle. Like Spartan, they realized that the tattoo test is the ultimate metric: when the product becomes the identity, the marketing is permanent and community-driven.

MONDAY MORNING PROTOCOLS

1. The Complexity Moat Search: Identify the cow pasture parts of your business, the areas that are easily copied. How can you add verticality? What is the most difficult, high-stakes version of your service that only you can execute? Shift your focus toward the black diamond projects that make your competitors hesitate.
2. The Three-Tier Audit: Are you only selling one level of engagement? Ensure you have a gateway product that is fast and accessible, a middle bridge designed for skill-building, and a destination summit so difficult and high status that only your top 1 percent achieve it.
3. The Identity Anchor: Look at your customer experience. Are people signing your Wall of Valor? Is your product tattoo-worthy? Ask yourself: if we stopped advertising tomorrow, would our customers still wear our brand to show they belong to the tribe? If not, you have a logo, but not a soul.

The Beast gave us the peak. By introducing a thirteen-mile mountain gauntlet, we had created a high-friction tier that validated our elite status and separated the high-resilience participants from the tourists. We had the Sprint (the entry point), the Super (the bridge), and the Beast (the summit).

But we noticed a lingering friction: once many racers finished their first event, they felt done. They had reached the summit, and their momentum was starting to plateau. They were exiting the system because they lacked a reason to stay. To keep the community moving, we needed more than just harder races; we needed a way to make the collection of races more valuable than the individual events themselves. We needed to transition from selling races to selling systemic completion. In 2012, we engineered what would become the most significant innovation in the company's history.

CHAPTER 15: THE TRIFECTA MACHINE

Hacking Psychology to Gamify Customer Retention

Most businesses treat a sale as the finish line. We treated it as an unclosed loop. By rewarding customers with an incomplete product—the Trifecta wedge—we shifted the focus from a single event to a season-long mission of completion.

THE BLUMA PROTOCOL

Weaponizing the Open Loop

In the 1920s, Soviet psychologist Bluma Zeigarnik sat in a bustling Vienna restaurant and noticed something strange: waitstaff could remember complex, unpaid orders perfectly, but the moment the bill was settled, the details vanished. The brain has a biological bias toward completion. An unfinished task creates a state of cognitive tension. Collaborating with legendary navigators of the mind like Vygotsky and Luria, she shifted her focus to broken machines, patients with brain injuries.

Her findings were a revelation for anyone trying to build a movement. She discovered that open loop tension is a hallmark of a high-performance engine; you only feel the itch to finish if your internal motivation is dialed in. Furthermore, she found that *mental homeostasis*—the need to close a loop—is what drives human achievement. This is the *Zeigarnik effect*. If you remove the friction of the unfinished task, you remove the drive to move forward.

THE WAR ROOM (THE LEAKY BUCKET)

Spartan HQ, Pittsfield, VT | January 2012 | Status: High Churn

The air was thick with stale coffee and overclocked laptops. Joe was pacing. "We're burning cash on acquisition," he barked. "We pay to find a customer, they run one race, and they disappear. We're a bucket with a hole in the bottom." Lorenzo, our analyst, pulled up the data. It was brutal: the one-

and-done rate was nearly 85 percent. People came for the experience, got the shirt, and checked the box. We were starting from zero every Monday morning. Matt Murphy suggested using the term *trifecta* (meaning a collection of three) from the ESPN broadcasts. It was a great word, but words don't stick to a refrigerator. We needed to gamify the struggle. The data showed that while one-race customers churned, three-race customers became lifers. We had to force the novice to become a lifer.

THE ANATOMY OF THE PIE

We didn't need new races; we needed to repackage the ingredients we already had. We categorized the Sprint as the red 5K entry drug, the Super as the blue 10K bridge, and the Beast as the green thirteen-mile monster. Individually, they were races. Together, they were a collection. To solve retention, we built hardware to match the rhetoric. We designed a revolutionary medal system: each race earned a standard medal plus a wedge. If you only did a Sprint, your shield was physically broken, a visual open loop staring at you from your trophy rack. You had to complete one of each to complete a Trifecta.

THE TRIFECTA: A RELIGIOUS RITE

This simple design choice hacked the most powerful psychological engine in the world: completionism. We saw the emergence of super-fanatics flying across the country just to get that final green Beast wedge. We weren't just selling tickets; we were selling the pieces of a soul. We ran a learning agenda with ten database segments to see what motivated people. For newbies, the motivation was discounts. But for returning racers, identity destroyed the discount. They didn't care about saving $20; they cared about the fact that they were one wedge away. The compulsion to complete the set was stronger than the desire to save money.

THE WALL OF FAME

To anchor this identity, Joe wanted to go big. We printed a massive towel featuring the names of every Trifecta earner in 6-point font. People would spend an hour searching for their name in the microscopic print just to take a photo. We had moved from selling a race to selling a ritual.

The statistical performance of the Trifecta gave us a massive friction advantage over the party mud runs of the era. While competitors suffered from an 85 percent initial churn rate, Spartan held a lower 65 percent rate because people returned specifically to finish their journey. Trifecta growth exploded by 200 percent year-over-year, and we started to bundle a Trifecta Pass to sell three tickets as one, increasing our average sale. By moving from disposable T-shirts to permanent identity signals like tattoos and medals, we turned a one-time participant into a lifer.

THE NAVIGATOR'S LOGIC

Incentive architecture requires an understanding of the psychological drain of narrative closure. When a customer checks the box, they exit your ecosystem. High churn is the tax you pay for a finished story. To maintain velocity, you must create an achievement gap by using physical anchors, like the Wedge Medal, to visualize a missing piece. You aren't selling a trophy; you are selling the empty space that needs to be filled. Leveraging the Zeigarnik effect allows you to ignite the spark of a completionist loop, turning a single event into a multi-stage mission. This shifts the focus from the cost of the transaction to the value of the transformation.

THE MARKET MIRROR: GARMIN

Garmin represents the definitive evolution from specialized navigation to comprehensive human engineering. While the brand began by mapping the world's terrain, it has spent the last decade mapping the internal terrain of the human engine. By 2026, Garmin has moved beyond the weekend warrior demographic to become the command center for the global performance elite. Over 45% of elite endurance athletes and a growing percentage of high-stakes corporate operators utilize Garmin's ecosystem to manage Operational Truth, anchoring the brand at the epicenter of the $610 billion longevity economy.

The platform's core value lies in its ability to quantify the "Body Battery"—a real-time measurement of physical and mental energy reserves derived from Heart Rate Variability (HRV), stress levels, and sleep quality. This provides a visceral, numeric representation of "Readiness" that forces the user to confront their biological reality.

Further driving the unfinished mindset is the Training Status algorithm. By categorizing effort into specific buckets like *Productive*, *Maintaining*, or the dreaded *Unproductive*, Garmin weaponizes the Zeigarnik Effect. It creates an open psychological loop; to a high-performer, seeing an Unproductive status is a piece of unfinished business that demands a systemic recalibration. By translating biometric data into a scoreboard for long-term sustainability, Garmin turns the daily routine into a high-stakes laboratory where the objective is the consistent maintenance of an unbreakable biological engine.

MONDAY MORNING PROTOCOLS

1. The Visual Void Audit: Look at your product offering. Does the customer feel finished after one purchase?

Design a three-part certification or a digital progress bar to trigger the psychological need for symmetry.
2. The Closure Campaign: Identify customers who have started but not finished a sequence. Send a communication that focuses on closure rather than a hard sale. Highlight that they are only a few steps away from completing the cycle.
3. The Earned Unlock: Define a reward that cannot be bought, only earned by completing a specific sequence. This turns your best customers into brand advocates who take pride in displaying the status they worked to achieve.

The Trifecta Machine was the breakthrough that turned Spartan into a year-long obsession. By 2012, we had the physics of completion working for us, but our operational environment was still the mountain. The mud and wilderness created a high-friction barrier for the urban masses. To achieve true global scale, we had to take the suck and flat-pack it into the heart of the city. We needed a venue that carried its own social gravity, a place where the history of struggle was already etched into the walls. We set our sights on the most iconic concrete in Boston, specifically the Green Monster.

CHAPTER 16: THE GREEN MONSTER

Infrastructure Hacking and the Urban Pivot

To achieve global scale, you must find a way to transport your core experience into environments where your customers already live.

THE CATHEDRAL BREAK-IN

Boston, Massachusetts | November 2012 | Pre-Dawn

The Green Monster is more than just a wall; it is a monument to the history of struggle. For a century, the greatest athletes in the world had faced their own personal beasts on this grass. But on a cold morning in November, home plate was covered in Spartan branding, and the sounds of baseball were replaced by the rhythmic thumping of thousands of sneakers hitting concrete. We had taken the Spartan phalanx out of the woods and marched it into the heart of the city.

It was just before 4:00 a.m. Fenway Park loomed large in the night, a brick-and-steel cathedral sitting silently in the biting mid-November air. It was the morning of the big event, and I was awake early. I decided to jog the three miles from the hotel to the venue rather than wait for the team to wake up. When I reached Gate D, it was locked tight. I stood for a moment debating the optics. I took a quick look over my shoulder, half expecting a Boston PD cruiser to roll up. Then I reached up, grabbed the ironwork, and started to climb. I laughed at the absurdity, scaling the gates of America's most beloved ballpark just to go to work.

I slipped over the wall and dropped into the shadows of the concourse. As I approached the security desk from the inside, I saw the guard. His head was back, mouth open, fast asleep. I didn't wake him. I didn't have the energy for an awkward conversation about why the race director was breaking into the park. I walked through the empty corridors and took a turn down a breezeway out to the stands to survey the scene, wondering how many people had ever stood inside the park all alone. Spartan tape marked a jagged course through the green seats. Sandbags were piled in the bleachers like bunkers. Heavy obstacles sat ominously on the warning track. And over the home plate circle, a massive Spartan banner lay flat like a declaration of war. We were about to do something that had never been done. Every venue has a rental fee, but Fenway's was in a league of its own, roughly ten times the cost of our mountains. If this worked, it would be a revolution. If it failed, it would be a spectacular, multi-million dollar disaster.

THE INTREPID PROLOGUE

Manhattan, New York | 2002 | Balance Bar Adventure Race Prologue on the USS *Intrepid* aircraft carrier

I yelled, "Safety check!" A technician gave my carabiners a final tug. "You're set." I looked down. The Hudson River awaited six stories below. My teammate Dave and I were standing on the flight deck of a massive warship, the USS *Intrepid*, about to rappel off the side. We climbed over the railing and leaned back, holding our descent with our brake hand. I let the rope slide through my worn gloves, hit the end of the line, which was still twenty feet off the water, and free-fell into the cold, dark water.

This was the prologue to the Balance Bar 24-Hour Race in 2002. By moving a dirt sport onto an iconic piece of military hardware in New York City, the organizers didn't just run a race; they created a news story. It proved that if you change the container of the struggle, you change the value of the brand. This lesson stuck with me when an opportunity came calling much later.

THE SCOUTING TRIP: BREAKING THE "NO"

The Stadium Series started with a cold call. Baseball stadiums sit empty approximately 270 days a year. They are massive assets with near zero revenue on off days. Initially, the Fenway staff suggested a Spartan Dash on the streets around the stadium. They could close off Lansdowne Street and hold an event with the park as the backdrop. We could line up several obstacles in a row and have a 100m dash, something I had wanted to try, but how much would people be willing to pay for that experience? As we walked the streets, I saw the back of the house area where deliveries came into the park, and it got me wondering, *What if we gave them the keys to the kingdom? What if we moved the race inside?*

They took me inside, which is always an exciting experience, with the lush green grass and iconic giant left field wall, affectionately known as the Green Monster, which they had to build due to the limited space in the city. The stadium had plenty of stairs, lots of rows of seats to run between, and a warning track we could place obstacles on. My dream was to have a giant cargo net climb up the Green Monster, but the head groundskeeper made it very clear early on that we could not touch the grass. As we walked through, I noticed a tour group. These were just ordinary fans and tourists who paid $40 just to go on the walking tour. If we combined a Spartan Sprint experience with the access, we could definitely make the economics work.

Joe was skeptical. To him, Fenway was just a clean box. He didn't follow sports; he had no idea what the Red Sox meant to Boston and felt that without the mud, the race lacked the soul of the mountain. He saw the astronomical rental fee and hesitated. I had to be the navigator of reality. "Joe", I argued, "in a stadium, we have built-in bathrooms, concessions, Jumbotrons, and house audio. In the woods, waste management is a margin killer. Here, the plumbing works. Most importantly: Fenway Park markets itself."

THE KEYS TO THE KINGDOM

We didn't just put a race in a park; we turned the park into an obstacle. Since Fenway is small, I clocked 2.7 miles of stairs, weaving back and forth between seats, encircling the triangle loading dock area, and walking the perimeter of the field on the warning track. We traded acreage for elevation. The groundskeeper nearly had a heart attack at the thought of a cargo net on his turf, so we pivoted: no one touches the grass. We used the warning track and the bleachers. We provided authentic access; we had racers doing pushups in the visiting locker rooms and sprinting past the Ted Williams Red Chair.

Fenway 2012 proved that the Spartan identity wasn't tied to mud, it was tied to effort. It opened the door to a massive urban demographic that wouldn't drive three hours to a mountain but would gladly take the subway to a stadium. In the world of consumer packaged goods, a product rarely remains static. We realized we had to apply the same logic. We offered the Sprint for the high-intensity enthusiast and the Beast for the endurance specialist. By moving from the wilderness into the Stadium Series, we were flat-packing the suck into the concrete cathedrals of urban sport. This wasn't just a marketing trick; it was strategic arbitrage. We were identifying residual gaps in iconic locations and filling them with a product that felt like it belonged there all along.

The first event was a massive success with almost eight thousand people. That lit the fuse to The Stadium Series. We have put on events in Dodger Stadium, Anaheim, Milwaukee, Raymond James, AT&T Stadium and Park, Citi Field, and more. Fenway Park remains a must attend event 15 years later.

THE NAVIGATOR'S LOGIC

In expansion, you will always face institutional resistance from gatekeepers who believe their environment is too sacred for your brand's intensity. Your job is to find the pivot that preserves their asset while enabling your mission. I call this contextual innovation – changing key elements of your product or service to create something new. When you lack horizontal distance, look for vertical displacement. In a stadium, you trade miles for metabolic load. Running on a remote mountain is a personal achievement, but running through Fenway Park is a credentialing story they will tell for a decade. Use high-status containers to grant your customers status. If you are short on space or resources, increase the intensity. This is the logic of going deeper rather than wider. Most businesses fail to scale because they believe their product is tied to a specific environment. By deconstructing your experience into its modular components, you can infrastructure hack existing environments to deliver your value at a higher volume.

MARKET MIRROR: RED BULL

Red Bull realized that sponsoring a local race was traditional corporate thinking, safe and invisible. Instead, they strategically integrated into iconic world landmarks like the cliffs of Santorini or the Opera House in Sydney. By changing the container of the stunt to a world-class stage, they turned a sugary drink into a global media empire. They moved the disruptive energy of the pirate into the cathedral of world tourism, borrowing the status of the location to validate the brand. They realized that the stage you stand on speaks as loudly as the performance you give.

MONDAY MORNING PROTOCOLS

1. The Sacred Space Identification: Identify the Fenway Park of your industry, a venue, platform, or partnership that currently feels off-limits. Look for a residual gap and negotiate for the time when the cathedral is dark and the owners are looking for supplemental revenue.
2. The Stairwell Math: If you are short on budget, time, or staff, increase the intensity of your current offering. How can you make your current service feel higher-stakes than a larger, flatter competitor? Go deeper into

the customer experience rather than wider into the market. Use contextual innovation to come up with a new offering.
3. The Keys to the Kingdom Offer: Identify one way you can give your customers an inside-the-shadows experience. Can you grant access to the visiting locker room of your process? People will pay a premium for the feeling of being somewhere they shouldn't be allowed.

The Green Monster proved that Spartan was a portable superpower. We had the mountains for the fanatics and the stadiums for the masses. We had built a brand that could survive in any environment. But as we looked at our growing empire, we realized that the manual override of the early years was becoming a liability. We were no longer a small group of raiders; we were a global institution. To survive the move from a scrappy brand to a permanent fixture, we had to face the ultimate friction of the corporate world: the transition of power and the discipline of the spreadsheet.

END OF PART III: THE SUPERPOWER

SURVIVING THE FRICTION OF 3,000 PERCENT GROWTH

By the end of year three, we had accomplished the impossible. We had built a continental footprint, survived the pressure of sixteen concurrent launches, and turned resilience into a game through the Trifecta machine. We had proven that a founding crew of dedicated disruptors could out-hustle the industry giants. But we had also reached the limit of individual heroics.

We had officially outgrown the pirate ship phase. If we stayed scrappy, we would stay small. To understand the mechanical pressure that forced this evolution, you have to look at the math of the scale.

In 2010, the genesis year, we ended with approximately 5,000 Spartans. We were a niche experiment, a special test in the Vermont woods. By the end of 2012, the explosion year, the Malibu event alone grew from 1,500 racers to over 9,000. Our total annual attendance surged to over 150,000.

This wasn't just more customers. It was a 3,000 percent increase in humanity, logistics, and liability in just twenty-four months. In the world of Two-Bike Math, this is the moment where the wheels usually fly off. Most companies shatter under this kind of success friction.

We survived because the Spartan operating system was finally online. The blueprint was locked, the teams were deployed, and the Trifecta machine was humming. We had survived the expansion. Now, we were about to enter the stratosphere.

The phalanx was no longer just a group of friends in a Vermont yoga studio; it was a global machine. But as we stepped out of the scrappy era, we realized that the final obstacle wasn't a mountain or a competitor—it was the transition from a movement into an institution.

THE INTERNAL SHADOW

By the end of 2013, the Spartan machine had finally become bulletproof. We had scaled past the point of no return, achieving a level of market dominance that seemed untouchable. But the man who helped build it was not. Throughout the relentless friction of the Forge, Scale, and expansion, a different kind of war had been quietly moving into the frame. While the world saw a superpower expanding across the globe, the biological cost of that effort was finally coming due. In the quiet moments between those final 2013 board meetings and the next global launch, I was forced back into a personal hurt locker that no amount of logic could solve. The machine we built was finally ready to run without its architect—just as the architect was forced into a war being fought not on a mountain, but inside his own cells.

INTERLUDE: THE NADIR

Vero Beach, Florida | January 2014

THE DIAGNOSIS

"Something's not right," said the dental assistant.
She stopped mid-procedure, set down her instruments, and went to get the dentist. She took one look inside my mouth — my gums were bleeding profusely and refusing to clot — and said four words that changed everything: "Go to the doctor. Now."

I had been feeling ill since Christmas. I assumed it was a standard winter bug working its way through the family. What wasn't standard was the purple bruise on the side of my right thigh. It looked like I had been struck by a tennis ball. I went to the clinic, they drew blood, and I went home.

The call came a few hours later.

"I think you have leukemia."

I wasn't prepared for that sentence. My brain started running calculations the way it always does under pressure, but none of the variables made sense. What does this mean? Am I going to die? Who do I call first?

My wife was in the car with our three children. I didn't want to panic her without more information. I called my brother-in-law, a physician, and read him the test results over the phone. He knew the head of oncology at Florida Hospital. I waited. The call came back within twenty minutes.

"The head of oncology recommends you check in to the hospital tonight."

I called my wife. She whipped the car around. On the ride over, we tried to explain to our kids that daddy was sick without saying more than we knew. We didn't know very much yet.

A normal white blood cell count is between 4,000 and 10,000 cells per microliter. Mine was over 50,000 — but they were non-functioning mimics. My body had manufactured a defective cell and begun replicating it with terrifying industrial efficiency. Counts over 20,000 generally carried bad outcomes. My brother-in-law met me at the front door and fast-tracked me into the cancer wing.

I had gone from a routine teeth cleaning to an ICU cancer patient by nightfall.

THE FIGHT

The diagnosis was acute myeloid leukemia. AML. The subtype with the lowest survival rate.

The treatment protocol was scorched earth. High-dosage chemotherapy kills everything — good cells and bad cells alike. Your white blood cell count drops toward zero. In that state, a simple cold can kill you. You live in a sterile bubble and wait for your body to decide whether it wants to rebuild itself.

Joe and Mike Morris came to visit. It was one of the few times I saw Joe truly off the clock. He brought a religious friend who performed a prayer session — awkward for a math-minded systems guy like me — but I was at zero count. I was willing to accept any fuel available to the engine.

I spent over two months in and out of the hospital for multiple chemotherapy sessions, combined with two to three doctor visits per week for infusions of platelets, blood, and Neupogen shots to rebuild my white blood cell count. I applied the only code I knew: accept it, do not quit, reroute when the map changes.

The map changed during my third round of treatment. A new doctor arrived with a new assessment. My current plan wouldn't work long-term. Without a stem cell transplant, he argued, I would relapse within two years. The medical community was in disagreement. My current doctor pushed back. Because so few people had survived AML at that stage, there was no reliable longevity data. I was fighting the illness and the experts simultaneously.

I did what any navigator does when the team can't agree on a route: I sought a third opinion.

The Moffitt Cancer Center in Tampa gave me the clearest read on the terrain. The data there was unambiguous. The transplant was the only vector that led to long-term survival. I updated the map and committed to the new course.

Finding a donor through the BeTheMatch registry took time. The match came back from Texas — a college student named Evan Burrough. He gave six hours of his life to a stranger so that stranger could keep his.

Back in the hospital, I underwent a fourth round of chemotherapy combined with a drug called ATG — formally known as "The Rabbit." It stops your body from attacking foreign cells, clearing the way for someone else's biology to take hold. The expected pain from this combination was unlike anything in the previous rounds. They hooked up a morphine drip and handed me a controller to release more if I needed it. I was about to hit the true zero count.

THE ZERO COUNT

For the first time in my life, I think I may die tonight.

I have paddled down Class IV rapids, rappelled off sheer cliffs, and been lost in the backwoods of Maine in the middle of the night, but never felt my life was in true danger until now.

Curled in a ball, staring at the inside rails of my ICU hospital bed filled with indicator lights, I think: this is how a lot of people die. In this position, in this room, maybe even in this bed — alone. The big procedure is tomorrow and it is clear to me now that I won't be able to sleep.

It seems crazy to have that much autonomy over substances I have never taken before, nor have any idea how they will affect me. I make up my mind that I will not press the button. I've been in pain before.

At 3:00am the alarm went off for the third time, sending the nurse rushing into my room ready to jump into action. The monitor indicated that my heart rate was critically low. Years of endurance training gave me a naturally low resting heart rate, and combined with the medicine swirling through my body, it had pushed me below thirty beats per minute. I came out of the fog long enough to say I was fine.

I just need to make it through the night. I have been here before — not in this room, not in this bed — but in this specific darkness. Racing for multiple days without sleep, dehydrated, mentally spent, you learn that the night lies to you. It tells you it won't end. It tells you to quit. We had a rule in adventure racing: no one quits during the night. The sunrise always changes the math.

I just need to survive until morning.

The transfusion the next day felt like a small fire coursing through my veins. When you receive a stem cell transplant, your entire immune system is reset. You are biologically reborn. The medical team counts your days from this new birthday. I was back at day one.

THE RETURN

In endurance racing, you don't measure a course in miles. You measure it in checkpoints. You don't think about the finish line when you're in the middle of the night. You think about the next marker. Get to that one. Then find the next.

The transplant worked the same way.

Day one was survival. Nothing more. The body in a sterile room, the machine continuing without me somewhere out there, Joe calling with ideas I couldn't execute yet. I kept my laptop open. I kept my phone charged. If I couldn't be in the field I could still be on the radio. I answered emails from the hospital bed. I took calls between infusions. The navigator doesn't abandon the map just because he can't walk the terrain.

Day seven was a different kind of checkpoint. The acute crisis had passed. The new biology was beginning its work. The sterile bubble held. I was still inside it but I could feel the walls of it more clearly now — which meant I could start calculating the distance to the edge.

The restrictions were precise and non-negotiable. No freshly cut grass — the bacteria in clippings could overwhelm a new immune system that had never encountered them before. No cold deli meat — listeria risk for a body that had no defenses yet. No crowds, no handshakes, wear a mask in public, no casual contact with the ordinary microbial world that healthy people move through without a second thought. My body was a newborn in a grown man's frame. I retook every childhood vaccination from scratch.

Day one hundred was the diagnostic checkpoint that mattered most. At one hundred days the vitiligo appeared — white spots across my skin, my immune system attacking the foreign cells that Evan Borough's donation had introduced. Most people would see a disfiguring side effect. My doctor saw a confirmation.

"You are cured," he said. "The vitiligo is a sure sign the process is working." No doctor had ever been so bold to say such a thing.

The reintegration was gradual in the way that a navigator re-enters a race after a forced stop — carefully at first, testing each footfall, then with increasing confidence as the terrain proves stable. The first time I walked outside without calculating the risk. The first time I sat in the grass without thinking about it. The first cold sandwich. Small checkpoints that healthy people cross without noticing, each one a finish line to me.

Throughout all of it — the rounds of chemotherapy, the donor search, the transplant, the hundred-day vigil, the slow reentry — I never fully left the field. My laptop and phone were always open. The Spartan machine kept running and I kept my hand on it from whatever room I was in. I don't say that to sound heroic. I say it because the work was part of the medicine. Having a mission to return to gave the body a reason to rebuild.

The machine didn't stop while I was gone. Here is what it became.

THE SUPERPOWER MANIFESTO

SCALE THE SUFFERING

To transition from an insurgent brand to a global institution, you must carry the Four Laws of the Superpower with you:

1. Strategic Integration: You stop building from scratch. You look for "cathedrals": Stadiums, ski resorts, and global platforms, which have already solved the plumbing and the parking, so you can focus entirely on the intensity.
2. The Complexity Moat: You recognize that "easy" is a commodity. You intentionally seek out the high-friction "black diamond" slopes because the competition is too soft to follow you into that level of operational difficulty.
3. The Transformation Logic: You realize your product isn't a race; it's a life-saving pivot. Whether it's a seven-hundred-pound man or a burnt-out CEO, you aren't selling tickets—you are selling a rebirth.
4. Status Architecture: You move from "product features" to identity. You realize that a permanent tattoo is a more accurate metric of brand health than a satisfaction survey.

THE END OF THE BEGINNING

The founding era is complete. You have achieved total territorial dominance. You have the Trifecta engine driving retention and the Stadium Series driving urban scale.

But as you reach the zenith, the stakes change. It is no longer about surviving the scale; it is about governing the category. We are moving from building the machine to an unbreakable legacy.

The unregulated era is over. We'll see how the virus of Spartan DNA infected everything from foreign royalty to the Olympic committee, and how the friction advantage faced its ultimate test: a world that was about to stop moving entirely.

PART IV: THE LEGACY

Transitioning from a Movement to a Global Institution

The final evolution of a brand is the transition from a *what* to a *how*. It is the moment when the founder's magic becomes invisible and the logic becomes universal.

By the end of 2013, the Nomadic Phalanx had achieved the impossible: a continental footprint, licenses in twenty countries, and the birth of the Trifecta engine. But we had also reached the limit of individual heroics. A brand built solely on raw intensity eventually hits a ceiling. To achieve true global dominance—to reach the Olympic stage—we had to move from Building the Machine to Governing the Category.

THE ARCHITECTURE OF OUTLASTING

To transition from an insurgent brand to a global institution, the Superpower Laws we forged during the scale-up now had to become our permanent Operating System. This required the standardization of suffering. We had to package our chaotic energy into a machine that delivered the exact same value proposition in a London stadium as it did on a Vermont farm. If your product requires the founder's magic touch to be successful, it isn't a business, it's a cult. Global legacy is achieved the moment you turn your subjective experience into an objective standard that the world cannot live without.

THE ZENITH AND THE LEGACY

The founding era is complete. You have achieved total territorial dominance. But as you reach the zenith, the stakes change. It is no longer about surviving the scale; it is about protecting the legacy.

In this final phase, we move beyond the mud and the medals to see how the Spartan DNA infected everything from foreign royalty to the Olympic Committee. We will witness Spartan face its ultimate existential test: a global Red Wedding moment where the world was about to stop moving entirely, and the system we built was all that remained.

CHAPTER 17: THE GLOBAL SUPERPOWER

A Movement Is Only as Strong as Its Infrastructure

To transition from a niche obsession to a global category, you must eventually embrace institutional gravity and turn your subjective magic into an objective platform.

THE CORPORATE INVASION

Ft. Lauderdale, Florida | 2013 | Status: Institutional Gravity

It was 90 degrees. The fairways of the pristine golf course were crawling with large iguanas. They scurried across the greens, looking confused by the walls and barbed wire we had erected on their manicured home. Each time a group of athletes ran past, the reptiles scattered for cover. I stood at the finish line holding a *pugil stick*—a padded weapon used in bayonet training. After Race Directing the special event, the final job of the day was to play the role of gladiator for the final two runners on the course.

Runner 1 was Swizz Beatz, the legendary hip-hop producer. I gave him the Hollywood treatment, a gentle tap on the shoulder as he crossed the line. Runner 2 was Joe De Sena. I gripped the stick tighter. Joe wasn't just my boss; he was the architect of four years of sleepless nights, near bankruptcies, and a frequently broken spirit. I didn't see a CEO; I saw a target. I swung with the full weight of my frustration. *Thwack.* I connected solid, sending him stumbling into the dirt. He looked up, wiping sweat from his face, and grinned. "Felt like you were letting something out there," he said. "Yeah," I replied. "Four years of torture."

This wasn't a normal race. It was a private retreat for Reebok. Their CEO was there along with the entire upper management for a launch party. We were no longer in the woods of Vermont eating raw onions; we were in the VIP tent of global commerce. But a VIP tent doesn't scale. To conquer the globe, we needed infrastructure.

THE REEBOK UNIFORM AND THE NBC MEGAPHONE

The partnership with Reebok was the rocket fuel that turned our campfire into an atmospheric inferno. It was a massive, multi-year deal that gave us Global Retail Infrastructure. Suddenly, Spartan gear wasn't just in a muddy tent; it was in malls from London to Tokyo. This marriage created institutional friction: guidelines, lawyers, and standard operating procedures. Some of the original nomads hated it, fearing the soul was being sold. I saw it as the necessary armor for a global campaign.

If Reebok was our uniform, NBC was our megaphone. Bringing Spartan to national television changed the stakes. We stopped timing anonymous racers and started directing characters. We highlighted Amelia Boone (The Assassin), the high-powered attorney; Hobie Call (The Blue Collar Hero), the HVAC installer; and Hunter McIntyre (The Sheriff), the larger-than-life personality. When the red light on the cameras went live, we moved into the mainstream sports conversation.

Then came the cultural crossover. It started with NFL legends like Randy Moss and moved to global icons like Serena Williams and Alicia Keys. Finally, it escalated to the royal family. Seeing Prince Harry associated with the zeitgeist was the ultimate coronation when we created a special course for him and James Corden. It confirmed that the suck wasn't a niche obsession; it was a universal language.

THE WORLD STAGE AND THE MACHINE

By 2014, the Spartan machine had achieved total market synchronization. We deployed four separate regional fleets in the US, each consisting of six eighteen-wheelers packed with standardized kits. This was a mobile operating system that could be dropped into any terrain and be race-ready in forty-eight hours. We exported the DNA into forty different countries. By 2018, the international business accounted for 50 percent of our total racers.

We had standardized the suck so that a burpee in Sparta felt the same as a burpee in Seattle. We outlasted rivals who faltered or pivoted away from the high-friction model. Every event felt like a victory lap. We had outpaced the market to the point that invincibility seemed like a permanent state.

THE NAVIGATOR'S LOGIC

Transitioning from a cult to a culture requires the platform pivot. You don't lose your soul by wearing a uniform; you gain the supply lines necessary to win a global war. In the attention economy, you must treat character as content. Mass media requires faces to root for, not just finishers to count. Furthermore, embrace standardization as scale. The burpee became our Big Mac, the universal unit of measurement that guaranteed quality regardless of geography. Finally, recognize the liability of size. Institutional dominance provides velocity, but the biggest machines are the hardest to park when the environment changes overnight.

THE MARKET MIRROR: THE UFC

In the 1990s, the UFC was a pirate event—unregulated, banned from cable, and operating in the shadows. To become a global superpower, they embraced institutional gravity. They standardized the rules, partnered with global giants like ESPN, and moved from underground brawls to a regulated sport. Like Spartan's Reebok moment, they traded unrestricted freedom for market dominance. They realized that to change the world, you have to be invited into its living rooms.

1. The Character Audit. NBC didn't just film people running through mud; they filmed an attorney and an HVAC installer conquering their own limitations. They sold characters, not just finishers. This week, audit your outward-facing content to see if you are selling the specs of your product or the transformation of the person using it. Identify three characters within your customer base and stop marketing your features. Instead, start narrating their friction. If you aren't telling the story of the struggle, you aren't building a tribe; you're just running a catalog.

2. The Shrapnel Stories. New employees often only see the cathedral, the global deals, the polished offices, and the scale. They didn't see the shrapnel, the broken trucks, the days payroll almost bounced, and the raw friction of the forge. At your next team meeting, don't talk about a win. Tell a story about a catastrophic failure and exactly how the team navigated the heat to survive. Remind your people that the institutional armor they wear today was earned in the dirt, not granted in a boardroom. Legacy is maintained by those who respect the scars of the origin.

3. The Big Mac Test. The burpee became the Spartan Big Mac, the universal unit of measurement that guaranteed the same "suck" in London as it did in Seattle. Standardization is the only way to scale without losing the soul of the machine. Identify the one core value or standard of your product that must remain identical across every geography or department. If you stepped out of the room today and that standard would fail to hold up without your magic touch, you haven't built a business; you've built a job that depends on your presence. True scale is the ability to walk away from the machine and know the gears will keep grinding exactly as you intended.

THE SUCCESS TRAP

Invincibility is a dangerous data error.

From 2015 to 2019, Spartan was finally flush with cash. We had solved the corporate friction and fortified our logistics; we felt untouchable. Joe bought back shares from early investors, reclaiming total control of the wheel. We went on an aggressive acquisition spree, buying up trail races, endurance events, and eventually our primary rival, Tough Mudder. We were no longer just a startup; we were a global Juggernaut with a massive, hungry infrastructure.

But success creates its own kind of institutional weight. The greatest disruption we would ever face wasn't on our risk matrices. It was a biological black swan. The 2020 lockdowns didn't just create a hurdle; they incinerated the very foundation of our business: mass human gathering. Our eighteen-wheelers, stadium contracts, and newly acquired assets became massive liabilities overnight. To survive, we had to strip away the institutional armor and return to the forge.

CHAPTER 18: THE VIRUS

Engineering Survival: How Existential Necessity Forced the Birth of Decentralized Innovation

Most marketing is a transaction, you pay for an impression, and the momentum dies the moment the check clears. A virus is different; it is a self-replicating asset that gains velocity as it spreads. For Spartan, the infectiousness of the brand is directly tied to the difficulty of the experience. When the customer becomes the salesperson, you have achieved the ultimate competitive state: a brand that grows while you sleep.

THE RED DOTS

Vero Beach, Florida | February 2020 | Status: The Death Sentence

I remember the exact moment the realization hit me: *This is bad.*

I was in Vero Beach. The sun was shining, and the ocean was calm. But the news flashing across my phone was apocalyptic. The red dots on the global infection map were spreading like wildfire across a dry prairie.

The recommendations quickly became mandates: "Stay away from people. No gatherings. No crowds. For a company that sold the experience of thousands of people sweating, bleeding, and breathing on one another, it wasn't just a hurdle; it was a death sentence.

We began to postpone events one after another. If we didn't do it, the venues were calling us to say that they could not host the events. Customers were reaching out asking what was going to happen. No one had answers.

THE "RED WEDDING" CALL

Google Hangout | March 2020 | Status: Total Silence

The calendar invite appeared with no agenda. When I logged on, the screen was a mosaic of hundreds of anxious faces. Joe didn't have a list of names. He just delivered the blunt, surgical reality: "The sky is closed. We cannot run events. We have to make drastic cuts immediately."

The chat box exploded. My phone started vibrating off the desk: "Am I safe?" "Are we going under?" I didn't have answers. I was just another face in the grid, watching a decade of momentum hit an immovable object.

THE REFUND PLEA

The Cash Crunch

We were facing an existential math problem. We had millions of dollars in ticket revenue for events that legally couldn't happen. If everyone demanded a refund today, Spartan would cease to exist tomorrow. We recorded a raw video appeal to the community: "If that $100 is existential to you, take it back. But if you can afford to wait, please hold your ticket. It's existential to us."

To their credit, the tribe held the line. But we were on life support. We needed a new special test. Necessity was no longer a mother; it was a drill sergeant.

THE LAB: MURDERING THE PLAN

Abandoned Kmart, Denver, CO | Early 2020 | Status: Skunkworks

The origin of our survival strategy wasn't a boardroom; it was an abandoned Kmart. Months earlier, Joe had explored acquiring HYROX, a European company staging fitness events that combined running and exercises in an indoor setting. When the deal fell through, Joe's reaction was classic Spartan: spite innovation. "If we can't buy them, we'll out-build them." Yancy Culp and Jarod Cogswell rented a 150,000-square-foot abandoned Kmart in Denver. It was freezing, with snow leaking through the roof.

We used that space to iterate the event format and created DEKA FIT: ten zones of exercise, each preceded by a 500-meter run. They brought in elites like Robert Killian to test the movements. When Ryan Kent clocked a 29:58 time trial, we had our benchmark. We knew we had an event that would challenge elite humans while remaining accessible to the masses. We were engineering a lifeboat out of plywood and fluorescent lights.

The event was defined, and the first big launch was planned for March 2020. Over seven hundred people were signed up by February, just as the world started to shut down.

THE LIFEBOAT: EVENT IN A BOX

Florida | Summer 2020 | Vero Strength and Conditioning Gym

When the pandemic hit, DEKA went from a side project to a survival strategy. We became nomadic, loading equipment into rental vans and shifting to Florida, where gyms were reopening faster. We created DEKA STRONG: an indoor version that removed the running component to fit inside local gyms.

Gym owners were dying. I realized we couldn't host five thousand people in a stadium, but we could help a gym owner host fifty people in a warehouse. We could provide the rules, the marketing, the collateral, and the leaderboard, and they could help us generate revenue. This was the event in a box. We would split the revenue, providing a vital lifeline to the small business owners while creating a network of affiliates who would drive business back to us when the world reopened. It was a massive win-win that caught on quickly.

THE FEMALE PIVOT

Celebrate vs. Suffer

As we rolled out DEKA, we noticed a massive demographic shift. While Spartan OCR was typically 70 percent male, DEKA sat at a perfect 50/50 split. By removing the mud and the intimidation of the mountain, we had lowered the barrier to entry. This caused internal friction. Joe wanted to keep the soul hard. I wanted to celebrate fitness. I ignored the pushback. We shifted the tone from dying to thriving, and the market responded to the innovation of inclusion.

THE EFFICIENCY RATIO

The biggest revelation of DEKA was the shift in unit economics. We moved from a heavy, logistics-bound organization to a nimble model designed to scale quickly without the drag of physical infrastructure.

- Cycle Time: The obstacle course race [OCR] requires twelve days for build, race, and strike. DEKA requires only one day. Velocity increases when you reduce friction to increase frequency.
- Variable Cost: OCR involves high travel and machinery costs. DEKA uses convention centers, local staff, and fixed gear, protecting margins by eliminating acts-of-God risks like weather.
- Scalability: OCR growth is linear (one team equals one race). DEKA is exponential, utilizing over five hundred affiliates hosting multiple events per year each with 50-100 people. Leverage comes from using partners to scale the brand.

THE NAVIGATOR'S LOGIC

This is about decoupling pain from performance. When a setback like a global shutdown occurs, most people spend their energy lamenting. The navigator skips the lamentation and moves straight to action. Innovation is the byproduct of having no other choice. DEKA helped save the brand by turning Spartan into a distributed system. It proved that the suck could be standardized, flat-packed, and shipped in a box.

This system is now a fast-spreading virus that creates a flywheel for the brand. Gym owners see the benefit of affiliating with Spartan, as it brings people to their door. The more affiliates there are, the more people come to the DEKA events. When we have large DEKA events, more gym owners want to become affiliates.

MARKET MIRROR: ETSY

The Distributed Engine

In the mid-2000s, e-commerce was a centralized landscape dominated by giants like Amazon. The friction for a solo maker to reach a global audience was massive. Etsy didn't try to be a retailer; they engineered a distributed network. By providing the blueprint, the store infrastructure and payment rails, to individual makers, they turned their customers into their primary growth engine. They didn't build a store; they built a platform that enabled thousands of stores. They turned a necessity for income into a global innovation of micro-entrepreneurship.

MONDAY MORNING PROTOCOLS

Decentralizing the Core

1. The System-in-a-Box Drill: If your main distribution channel (store, website, or event) disappeared tomorrow, how would you deliver value? Identify your atomic unit, the core value you provide. Shrink your entire business logic into a single playbook that a stranger could operate. Prototype that manual this week.

2. The Host Strategy: You don't need to own the real estate; you just need to integrate with the people who do. Identify three partners who already have your customers but need your standard. Create a licensing-lite version of your service where they keep the majority of the revenue but use 100 percent of your DNA.
3. The Asset-Light Test: Identify your heaviest asset (lease, equipment, servers). How could you deliver the same result if you removed that asset from your balance sheet tomorrow? Shift your mindset from operator to certifier.

The pandemic was a forced audit of our soul. It stripped us of the eighteen-wheelers and the stadium lights, leaving us with nothing but the code and a community that refused to stop moving. We proved we could survive as a virus: decentralized, modular, and resilient. But as the world began to reopen, a digital leaderboard wasn't enough. The tribe didn't just want to track their output; they wanted to feel the mud.

We were no longer just the machine or the pirates. We had become a hybrid. We were returning to the mountains not just to run a race, but to cement a legacy that could survive anything—even a global halt. This survival had refined our logic: if we could systematize the struggle to work in a locked-down garage, we could standardize it to work on the world's most prestigious stage. The virus had given us the speed; now the superpower was ready to claim the ultimate institutional prize.

The path from the Vermont hayfield was leading to a new, five-ringed horizon.

CHAPTER 19: THE OLYMPIC ASCENT

Institutionalizing Grit: The Transition from Disruptive Rebellion to Recognized Authority

Transitioning from a trend to a sport requires moving from a brand name people buy to a set of rules the world lives by.

THE BROADCAST (FUTURE STATE)

Los Angeles Memorial Coliseum | August 2028 | Status: Mainstream

BROADCASTER 1: "Welcome back to the LA Coliseum! We are live for what promises to be one of the most exciting events of the summer: The Modern Pentathlon Obstacle Course!"

BROADCASTER 2: "Just a few years ago, this was unthinkable. Pentathlon used to be horses and fencing. But the inclusion of the Obstacle discipline has brought a new level of raw grit to these Games."

(SOUND of starter pistol)

BROADCASTER 1: "And they are off! Team USA's Sarah Chen explodes into the Inverted Wall! A classic Spartan-style climb!"

BROADCASTER 2: "She's flying over the Atlas Stones! This isn't just a footrace, Jim. This is a battle against gravity, fear, and friction. These athletes have bridged the gap between traditional Olympic discipline and the primal challenge of the obstacle course."

The meeting in that Hartford coffee shop felt like a lifetime ago. Back then, we were just trying to convince five hundred people to pay us to crawl in the mud. Now, the world was watching. We hadn't just built a company; we had engineered a new Olympic discipline. But getting to that coliseum didn't start with a grand vision of gold medals; it started with a profound fear of disappearing.

THE FAD FEAR: FROM TREND TO FIXTURE

Joe was always haunted by the word *fad*. In the hyper-growth years, his greatest fear wasn't failure—it was irrelevance. He knew that for Spartan to survive the friction of time, it had to move from a weekend challenge to a permanent sport. The lightbulb clicked when Joe found archival photos of French athletes from the early twentieth century using military-style obstacles. The logic was instant: if the foundations of athleticism were built on obstacles, then Spartan isn't a new invention, it's a homecoming. But realizing you belong in the history books and actually getting the International Olympic Committee (IOC) to recognize the discipline are two very different diplomatic challenges.

THE NAVIGATOR'S QUEST: THE BUREAUCRATIC GAUNTLET

In 2013, the request hit my desk: "Research what it takes to get a sport into the Olympics." At the time, we were still figuring out the logistics of portable toilets. The research revealed a bureaucratic structure more daunting than any Death Race. To the IOC, you don't just show up with a brand. You have to build a global governing system, including global proliferation (forty countries on three continents), an independent federation (national governing bodies), and an international federation (IF) to handle anti-doping and rules.

We needed a specialist. Enter Ian Adamson. Ian was my original adventure racing hero. Now, we were partners. Before Ian could sell the world on the bureaucracy, we had to prove the physics of the format.

JERRY WORLD: THE LABORATORY

AT&T Stadium, Dallas, TX | 2013 | Status: The Big League

Long before the torch was lit, we needed a laboratory to prove the concept. I stood on the fifty-yard line of AT&T Stadium on the Dallas Cowboys star, the video board hanging over the turf like a spaceship. Ian and I had constructed an event designed to mimic a future Olympic format, courting the USA Pentathlon. We designed a short course: two blistering laps of obstacles, interrupted by a laser pistol station. Shooting with laser pistols was an element in the Modern Pentathlon, we wanted to demonstrate the integration. The challenge was the Laser Protocol: race at 180 beats per minute, then instantly freeze your body for a precision shot. It was fast, visual, and TV-ready.

THE ARCHITECT'S VOICE (EGO DEATH)

The hardest friction wasn't technical; it was ego. Joe De Sena does not like the word "no." He wanted the Spartan helmet on the Olympic podium. Ian Adamson had to be the architect of reality. "Joe," he explained, "you can't have 'Spartan' in the Olympics any more than you can have 'Ironman' in the Olympics. Ironman is a brand; triathlon is the sport."

We had to implement a white-label strategy. We built a neutral federation (World Obstacle) and promoted OCR (obstacle course racing) as a discipline. If we controlled the global standards, Spartan would naturally become the Ironman of the sport, the premium brand within a recognized global system. It felt like we were being asked to erase our names from our own invention, but the logic was sound.

THE REBOOT: THE SAINT BOY INCIDENT

In 2021, history threw us a bone. In Tokyo, a German pentathlon coach was filmed striking a horse named Saint Boy when it refused to jump. The world exploded in outrage. The IOC gave modern pentathlon an ultimatum: replace the horse, or you are out of the Games. The door cracked open because the existing structure was failing. We provided the solution.

In 2026, it was decided that obstacles were going to replace the horse jumping portion of the Modern Pentathlon competition at the 2028 Olympics in Los Angeles.

THE NAVIGATOR'S LOGIC

To achieve the maximum scale of an idea, the creator must often become invisible through a strategic white label. By stripping the Spartan name away for the Olympics, we ensured the survival of the standard. Understand that bureaucratic obstacles are just another mountain; you don't outrun a glacier, you navigate its pressure points through diplomatic endurance. Finally, master the Laser Protocol: high-performance discipline is the ability to move from maximum physical output to absolute mental stillness. This is the unbreakable mind in its purest form.

MARKET MIRROR: THE WORLD SURF LEAGUE (WSL)

Surfing was once a fragmented soul-sport culture with no centralized authority. The WSL moved in and standardized judging, created a professional global tour, and built the governing infrastructure required for Olympic inclusion. Like Spartan, they realized that the Olympic ascent is the final act of the friction advantage. It turns a localized subculture into a permanent global institution by adopting the rules of the establishment to gain the reach of the entire world.

MONDAY MORNING PROTOCOLS

1. The Legacy vs. Logo Audit: Ask your leadership team: "If we achieved our ten-year vision but our company name was erased from history, would we still do it?" If the answer is "no," you are building a monument to yourself, not a mission. Identify one partnership you walked away from because you wouldn't get enough credit, and reconsider its scale potential.
2. The Category King Rewrite: Stop selling your features; start selling the result. Rewrite your core value proposition to own the benefit. Don't sell "accounting software"; sell "audit-proof peace of mind." Make your brand the synonym for the result.
3. The Broadcast Format Test: What part of your product is too messy or complex for the mass market? Design a "broadcast version" of your offering. Simplify the format to amplify the reach.

We have reached the coliseum. We have navigated the border crossings, the mud pits, the boardrooms, and the global lockdowns. We have proven that the friction advantage is the only true competitive moat in a world that seeks the easy path. But as any navigator knows, the story doesn't end at the finish line. It ends with the person you became while you were navigating the storm. You have moved through the prototype, the expansion, and the institution. It's time for the final word. It's time to remain unbreakable.

CHAPTER 20: THE FRICTION ADVANTAGE

In a world obsessed with frictionless living, the ultimate competitive advantage belongs to those who seek out the resistance. Most leaders view friction as a loss of energy, a drag on the system to be engineered away. They are inadvertently building for atrophy. The Spartan knows that friction is the source of the spark.

THE GENERATIONAL FLYWHEEL

Broward County Convention Center, FL | December 2025 | Status: Full Circle

The air inside the massive hall was electric, thick with the scent of high-performance rubber and the collective nervous energy of a thousand elite athletes. The lighting was cinematic, sharp blues and oranges cutting through the cavernous space, punctuated by the rhythmic clack-clack of rowers and the heavy thud of medicine balls. I stood at the finish line. From this vantage point, the floor looked like a high-speed circuit board. This was the mountain-in-a-box we had conceptualized during the dark days of the pandemic.

A young man in a sweat-drenched jersey approached me. He was twenty-two, with the lean, functional build of a machine. "Brian?" he gasped. He reached into his gym bag and pulled out a small, laminated photo. "I've been waiting to show you this." It was a picture from 2010. A muddy kid, maybe seven years old, wearing a Spartan Kids medal that was half the size of his torso. Standing next to him was his father, both grinning like they'd just conquered Everest.

"That's me," he said. "That race changed my life. My dad didn't just want me to run; he wanted me to learn that the hardest path is usually the right one. Today, I just hit a sub-thirteen-minute DEKA Strong." I looked out at the rows of athletes. The data and the logistical nightmares of the last two decades vanished. I wasn't thinking about the permit battles or the "Red Wedding" calls. I was looking at a generational flywheel.

THE ARCHITECTURE OF SUCCESS (CHAOS AS FUEL)

Success in the modern era is rarely a solo act; it is a convergence of forces. We didn't just work hard, we harnessed the CrossFit catalyst and the social media force multiplier. However, the engine of that growth was Joe's systemic volatility. While the lack of resources and the sixteen-point expansion were blindingly stressful, they were necessary. Chaos is the ultimate filter; it strips away the indecisive and forces the remaining team into a state of adaptive velocity. We survived the pandemic not because we were comfortable, but because we were experts at being uncomfortable. That required comfort with discomfort is exactly how you must approach the unknown tools of the future.

THE AI PIVOT (DIGITAL LEVERAGE)

There is always a new way to create friction, and a new way to solve it. Take artificial intelligence. Throughout the writing of this manuscript, I used AI as a modern-day Two-Bike Math. It is the ultimate digital lever. It helped organize the chaos of twenty years of memories into a deployable narrative. Some fear the tool; Spartans use the tool. It is an OODA loop accelerator. It allows you to orient and decide faster than the competition.

> The Navigator's Note: The tool is not the work. You still have to provide the sweat. The tool identifies the path, but the character is built in the movement.

THE SOUL IN THE STRUGGLE

The central thesis of my life, forged in the unregulated era of adventure racing, is that friction is a positive force. In a world obsessed with making everything frictionless, one-click purchases and seamless deliveries, we are losing the very thing that builds character. Adventure racing taught me that struggle is the ultimate laboratory for the soul. It reveals who you are when the Sleep Monster arrives at 3:00 a.m. When you remove the struggle, you remove the revelation. By productizing that struggle, we gave millions of people the

chance to find a version of themselves they actually liked—
one that was unbreakable.

THE FINAL METRICS

Category	Metric	Impact
Total Reach	15,000,000+	Total humans who have crossed a Spartan finish line.
Retention	Thousands	Athletes with earned Trifecta shields (the closed loop).
Urban Scale	10,000+	Annual participants at the Fenway Park Stadium Race.
New Vector	200,000	Projected 2026 DEKA racers across ten countries.

THE NAVIGATOR'S LOGIC

Technology and comfort are depreciating assets. The only
value that appreciates over time is the ability to do hard things.
If your business solves a temporary technical problem, you are
vulnerable; if it solves the permanent human problem of
softness, you become eternal. You must choose to be the
whetstone rather than the pillow.

The modern obsession with seamless living represents the
drag of a comfort crisis. Fragility is the hidden tax we pay for a
life without resistance. To build a factory for resilience, you
must introduce the heat of voluntary hardship, deliberately

choosing one difficult task every day that you aren't required to do. This intentional friction ignites the spark of anti-fragility. When the real storm hits, you won't just survive, you will thrive. You become the obstacle that the world has to go around.

They say you can't catch lightning in a bottle twice. That the first time is luck, and the second is a miracle. But after the Halt of 2020, we didn't wait for a miracle. We returned to the forge. We stripped the weight, found our azimuth, and forged a stronger vessel ourselves. Catching lightning once is a story for the pirates; catching it a second time is the proof of the machine.

MARKET MIRROR: MARCUS AURELIUS & THE STOICS

The Roman emperor Marcus Aurelius wrote *Meditations* while leading a war and dealing with a plague. His core tenet: "The impediment to action advances action. What stands in the way becomes the way." This is the ancient root of the friction advantage. The obstacle isn't a barrier; it's the path.

MONDAY MORNING PROTOCOL: DYNASTIC THINKING

1. The Final Vector (Tactical Reframing): The goal is not a life without problems; it is a life with better problems. The next time a crisis hits your desk, say "Good." "The server crashed? Good. We can rebuild for 10x scale." Train your brain to see friction as fuel.
2. The Child of the Customer Test: Identify a *futurist*, or someone under twenty-five who has zero attachment to your past. Ask them: "Will this product still matter in twenty years?" If you sell a trend, you will disappear. If you sell a human truth (resilience, health, community), you are solving a permanent problem. Pivot toward the human truth.

3. The One-Hundred-Year Starship: What is the one
    project you could start today that won't be finished for
    fifty years? Plant one tree this week that you will never
    sit under. This shifts your team from quarterly goals to
    a legacy mission.

We have reached the end of the log. The map is drawn, the
data is archived, and the protocols are set. You are Becoming
Spartan. The only question left is: Which mountain are you
climbing tomorrow?

THE UNBREAKABLE MANIFESTO

Friction is the status symbol of the future.

The world is getting easier. AI will do our thinking. Robots will do our lifting. Screens will do our living. In that world, Friction is the ultimate status symbol.

I. Seek the Suck

If you have a choice between two paths, take the one with the most resistance. That is where the growth is hidden.

II. Hold the Line

When the Sleep Monster arrives, don't negotiate. Your character is formed in the seconds after you want to quit.

III. Build the Phalanx

Surround yourself with people who don't ask, "Why?" but, "How far?"

IV. Remain Unbreakable

Success is temporary. Grit is permanent.

THE FINAL WORD

The race doesn't end at the finish line. It ends with the person you became while you were running. You have navigated the hayfields of Vermont, the boardrooms of Boston, and the dunes of Abu Dhabi. You have the OODA Loop, the trifecta logic, and the friction advantage.

The map is in your hands now. The establishment is watching, the pirates are cheering, and the mountain is waiting.

STAY UNBREAKABLE.

EPILOGUE: THE INTERNAL SPECIAL TEST

Why the Finish Line Is a Mirage and the Struggle Is the Only Permanent Home

The greatest threat to a high-output life is the illusion of the destination. Most people spend their lives working toward a point of total comfort, a finish line where the friction stops. But in the architecture of the forge, comfort is a stagnant pond. The moment you stop applying intentional resistance to your life and your business is the moment entropy begins its work. Resilience isn't a trophy you keep on a shelf; it's a muscle that begins to atrophy the second you stop lifting. Becoming Spartan isn't about winning a single race; it's about choosing to stay in the heat of the forge forever.

EPILOGUE: THE SKIN TRADE

Once upon a time, a man was walking through the woods when Death came upon him. Death was planning to take him then and there, but the man begged for his life, pleading that his adventure wasn't over. Death noticed the man's beautiful tan skin—a life lived under the sun and in the elements—and made an offer: "If you give me your skin, I will let you be for now."

The man made the trade. He accepted the scars, shed his outer layer, and kept his adventure going.

In the world of Spartan, we have a saying: The course is never what you expected. You can spend weeks scouting the terrain, mapping the elevation, and calculating the water stops, but the moment the starting pistol fires, the Two-Bike Math takes over. The river swells. The mud thickens. The Sleep Monster arrives early.

I have spent sixteen years building a global machine designed to teach people how to handle that friction. But *Becoming Spartan* is not just about corporate resilience; it is a tactical manual for survival. Joe De Sena focused on the lifestyle; I focused on the output. It turns out these principles serve individuals in their darkest zero-count moments just as well as they serve a CEO in a boardroom.

DAY 4,335

The transplant described in the Interlude was over 4,335 days ago. Since then, I have traveled the world, celebrated my thirtieth wedding anniversary, and watched my children graduate. I returned to endurance training and have won several adventure races. I continue to lead the DEKA innovation for Spartan, and I continue to have the occasional (and healthy) battle with Joe.

I didn't survive the ICU because of medical luck alone. I survived because the suffering I learned in the woods had armor-plated my psyche. When the course changed and the Sleep Monster came for me, I didn't mourn the map. I applied the code. I rerouted. I traded my skin to keep my adventure going.

THE FINAL CHECKPOINT

Becoming Spartan is the proof of the legacy. The world will tell you that catching lightning in a bottle twice is impossible. They'll say the first time was a fluke of timing—a cultural spark that happened to catch fire—and that the second was a stroke of fate. Don't believe them.

We didn't wait for the storm to provide; we returned to the forge, stripped the institutional weight, and forged a vessel strong enough to hold the strike for a generation. Catching lightning once is for the pirates. Catching it again—sixteen years later, in the hands of a man who started as a child in your tracks—is the proof of the machine.

The Spartan journey doesn't end when you cross the finish line. The finish line is just the beginning of the next loop. The race ends but the code remains. You now have the tools to take on your own Agoge.

Lead through essence.

The map is in your hands now. Go build your legacy.

AROO!

FIELD REPORT: THE BIOLOGICAL PROOF

By Andi H. (Racer #0012)

A crisis—whether a diagnosis, a global pandemic, or a market collapse—is not an endpoint; it is a mandatory reroute. In the mud of a Spartan race, we see this transformation in real-time. We see individuals conquering addiction, divorce, or grief. They don't come for a fun run; they come for the positive friction that allows them to reboot their internal operating system.

"I signed up for a Spartan Race because I was drowning," Andi recalls. "I was in an abusive marriage, I had lost everything financially, and I had lost all self-worth. That first race was so tough, but it gave me a strength I didn't know I possessed.

One morning, a butcher knife was held to my throat. I could feel the tip piercing my skin. My husband asked, 'How does it feel to be ten seconds from death?'

But I was calm. I did not panic. I knew I was resilient. Because of the grit I practiced on the course, I had the clarity to walk away and never look back. I didn't just finish a race; I took my life back."

Andi's story is the ultimate "Operational Truth." The weapon we build in the laboratory of the race is designed for the wars we fight at home.

THE INTEL CACHE: SOURCES & FURTHER STUDY

This manual was not written in a vacuum. The weapon is a composite of engineering logic, military strategy, and psychological grit. If you want to dive deeper into the black line of the pool or the redline of the boardroom, start with these primary sources.

I. PSYCHOLOGY & COGNITIVE FRICTION

Zeigarnik, Bluma. *On Finished and Unfinished Tasks* (1927).

- The Navigator's Audit: The foundational study of the open loop. Without Bluma's work, the Spartan Trifecta is just a piece of metal. This is the science of why your brain won't let you quit until the puzzle is complete.

Csikszentmihalyi, Mihaly. *Flow: The Psychology of Optimal Experience.*

- The Navigator's Audit: Essential for understanding high-friction cogitation. It explains how the intersection of high challenge and high skill creates the "flow" state we seek in the mud and the lab.

II. STRATEGIC OPERATIONS & THE OODA LOOP

Boyd, John R. *A Discourse on Winning and Losing.*

- The Navigator's Audit: Boyd was the ultimate navigator. His "OODA Loop" (Observe, Orient, Decide, Act) is the core operating system of this book. If you can't cycle through this loop faster than the market (or the cancer), you lose.

Richards, Chet. *Certain to Win: The Strategy of John Boyd, Applied to Business.*

- The Navigator's Audit: A brilliant translation of fighter pilot logic into corporate maneuvering. It explains how orientation is the most important part of the loop.

III. MANUFACTURING, TQM & LEAN LOGIC

Deming, W. Edwards. *Out of the Crisis.*

- The Navigator's Audit: The bible of Total Quality Management. Deming taught me that "Variation is the Enemy." In Spartan, we applied this to standardize the suck across forty countries.

Ohno, Taiichi. *Toyota Production System: Beyond Large-Scale Production.*

- The Navigator's Audit: The origin of Just In Time and The Five Whys. Ohno's work on *muda* (waste) is why we audit our vanity vectors and static friction.

IV. LEADERSHIP & THE PHALANX

Pressfield, Steven. *The Gates of Fire.*

- The Navigator's Audit: While technically historical fiction, this is the best deconstruction of the nomadic phalanx in existence. It captures the essence of leading through essence rather than rank.

Willink, Jocko and Babin, Leif. *Extreme Ownership.*

- The Navigator's Audit: The modern standard for leading from the front. It aligns perfectly with the Spartan DRI (Directly Responsible Individual) protocol.

V. ADVENTURE & SURVIVAL DATA

The Ironman Archive (Dave Orlowski Interviews).

- The Navigator's Audit: The origin story of the Two-Bike Math. Studying the first 1978 Ironman is a study in zero-count survival where the map didn't even exist yet.

Siff, MC and Verkhoshansky, Yuri. *Supertraining*.

- The Navigator's Audit: For the physics of the Spartan race. If you want to understand the bio-mechanical friction of a fifty-pound sandbag on a 30 percent incline, start here.

VI. DISRUPTIVE STRATEGY & INVESTMENT LOGIC

Gardner, David. *The Motley Fool Rule Breakers*.

- The Navigator's Audit: Rule-breaking isn't about being reckless; it's about disruptive non-conformity. Gardner's logic proves that the most valuable companies are those that actively break industry standard friction to build their own unique category DNA. In building Spartan, we applied this by ignoring the traditional race-promoter playbook and instead used software engineering logic to scale a global movement. This is the primary manual for the boardroom phalanx.

ACKNOWLEDGMENTS

No one summits a mountain alone. Behind every individual achievement is a phalanx of people who carried the sandbags, held the torches, and refused to let the standard slip. To the following people: you didn't just help me write a book; you helped me survive the course.

THE ANCHOR

- To my wife: You are the navigator behind the navigator. You drove in silence to the ICU, managed the sterile bubble of our home, and kept our family moving forward while my world was at zero count. I traded my skin to keep the adventure going, but I only had an adventure worth keeping because of you.

THE ORIGINAL PHALANX

- Steve Vadas & Dave Giampietro: My teammates from Team Guiness days and the brutal adventure racing courses where we first learned the physics of the suck. You bled with me when there were no cameras and no crowds. Thank you for holding the line during those three-hundred-mile dogfights. Steve, a special thank-you for your critical eye in helping edit this manuscript—ensuring the navigator remained as precise on the page as he was on the map.

THE LIFEBLOOD

- Evan Burrough: In 2014, you were a college student in Texas who stepped onto a bus and gave a cheek swab to a stranger. You didn't know me, and you didn't owe me anything. Yet you gave six hours of your life to a machine so that I could have another decade of mine. You are the ultimate definition of unbreakable. Thank you for being my 10-out-of-10 match.

THE CATALYST

- Joe De Sena: You are the most beautiful, frustrating, high-friction maniac I have ever met. You pushed me until I broke, then demanded I find a higher baseline. Thank you for the Tasmanian Devil energy that turned a vision in Vermont into a global movement. We didn't always agree on the details, but we always agreed on the mission.

THE PHALANX

To the Dorm Room Raiders and the master builders who turned pixels into mud:

- Matt Murphy: For finding the Trifecta logic and being the voice of the sport when the world was finally ready to listen.
- Ben Killary: For living in a tent in a condemned barbershop and carrying that photocopied AmEx into the night. You proved that audacity is the best currency.
- Dan Luzzi: For not quitting in that muddy Vermont parking lot in 2010. You went from a kidnapped intern to a cornerstone of the empire.
- Russell Cohen: For building the walls that millions climbed—including that first Wall of Valor. You gave the brand its physical soul.

THE INNER CIRCLE

- To my children and family: Thank you for being the first special test for these pages. To those of you who spent hours proofreading, catching my typos, and challenging my memories: you are the reason this manuscript is finally elite.

AROO.

THE SPARTAN CODE: EXECUTIVE SUMMARY

This roadmap synthesizes the Spartan Way of business and life, a philosophy forged in the mud of Vermont and scaled to the global stage. It documents the transition from a scrappy, gear-strapped startup to a world-class Olympic discipline.

PART I: THE FORGE (Mindset Under Duress)

- The Resourcefulness Ratio (Two-Bike Math): Success is not a function of the gear you own; it is a function of the engine you build. Achieving 100 percent of the mission with 66 percent of the resources separates the standard manager from the Spartan leader.
- The OODA Loop Crisis Response: In the fog of war, speed beats perfection. Strip away the drama, orient to the constraints, and decide with 70 percent data. Movement is the only cure for the Sleep Monster.
- The Speed of Forgiveness: Visionary velocity must always stay one step ahead of the permit paradox. If you wait for every green light, you never leave the driveway. Sometimes, the fine is the most efficient line item on the balance sheet.

PART II: THE SPARK (Hyper-Growth Tactics)

- Weaponize the Friction: While competitors race to the middle to make things easy, move to the extremes. Difficulty is a natural brand moat; the harder the experience, the more defensible the territory.
- Identity over Transactions: A ticket is a transaction; the Agoge is a transformation. Transactions expire; identities are permanent. Sell the rebirth, not the seat.
- Operational Piracy: Audacity creates its own gravity. Use manual, unscalable work, like raiding dorm rooms for social proof, to ignite the fire when you lack venture capital.
- The Gas Can Strategy: When the high-tech solution fails, douse the problem in gasoline by hand. The customer sees the brilliant legend; the founder smells like gas.

PART III: THE SUPERPOWER (Product Dominance)

- Vertical Differentiation: If the market is crowded on flat ground (distance), move to the mountains (verticality). Change the battleground to an environment where you are the master.
- The Zeigarnik Machine: Hacking human psychology through the missing piece. A broken shield (the Trifecta) creates a cognitive tension that drives higher retention than any discount or loyalty program.
- Contextual Innovation: See value where others see a No. By infrastructure hacking—moving from the

mountains to the stadiums—you unlock massive urban demographics using the world's existing plumbing.

PART IV: THE LEGACY (Resilience & Legacy)

- The 30-Burpee Law: Excellence requires a physical tax. Standardize the penalty for failure to ensure that the struggle is universal and the finisher currency is valid across the globe.
- Micro-Scale Decentralization: When the world shuts down (the virus), flat-pack the soul of the brand. DEKA proved that the Spartan code is portable; own the standard, not the dirt.
- Institutional Alignment: To achieve global dominance, trade the ego for the legacy. Move from a brand to a sport to secure a seat at the Olympic table.
- The Nadir Protocol: The code isn't just for business; it is for survival. When you hit a zero-count moment—whether bankruptcy or a medical crisis—lead through essence.

APPENDIX: THE SPARTAN CODE FIELD MANUAL

The "Break Glass" Tactical Toolkit

The following is a condensed execution guide. It transforms twenty-five years of Navigator's Logic into immediate actions. If your mission is stalled, find the corresponding chapter and execute the protocol.

PART I: THE FORGE (THE ANCESTRY OF GRIT)

CH 1: THE BLACK HOLE FILTER | The DRI Audit Assign a single name to your three most important projects. If more than one person is in charge, you have a vulnerability. A filter that catches nothing is a window; if you aren't repelling the wrong people, you are accumulating a crowd.

CH 2: OPERATIONAL PIRACY | The Habit Audit Identify one rule your company follows that is actually just a habit. Break it this week to test for efficiency. Most teams read the rules to see what they *have* to do; the pirate reads them to find out what they *didn't* say.

CH 3: THE STRESS LABORATORY | The Math Vector Translation Take your most emotionally charged business problem and rewrite it using only raw data. Strip the adjectives and the drama until it is a logic problem. Resilience is a calibrated baseline; solve for the variables, not the feelings.

CH 4: TWO-BIKE MATH | The Capacity Transfer Identify your top performer and your biggest bottleneck. Attach a "tow line" between them. Task the high-performer with systematizing their speed to pull the bottleneck forward. You don't need a 1:1 ratio of tools to people to maintain 100% velocity.

CH 5: THE SLEEP MONSTER | The Darkness Rule
Establish a lockout for major strategic pivots or firings after
5:00 p.m. Never make a permanent decision in a temporary
state of exhaustion. Wait for the dawn to calibrate your
chemistry.

CH 6: THE SACRIFICIAL LAMB | The Catastrophe Filter
Identify tasks currently waiting for approval. If executing
without permission won't land you in jail or bankruptcy,
execute today. You can fix a messy launch; you cannot fix a
launch that never happened.

**PART II: THE SPARK (BOOTSTRAPPING THE
REVOLUTION)**

CH 7: THE COFFEE SHOP COUP | The Napkin Audit Distill
your fifty-page business plan onto a single 3x5 card. If you
cannot explain the "Niche Wedge"—the one thing you do that
the market leader is too slow or too soft to do—you are hiding
in complexity.

**CH 8: THE PROTOTYPE TEST | The Shovel Handle
Solution** Identify a project stalled by the lack of a
"professional" tool. Build a pirate version today, a low-cost,
functional prototype that allows you to start testing the logic
immediately. Perfection is the enemy of the first one hundred
customers.

CH 9: DORM ROOM RAIDERS | The Social Gravity Hack
Identify where your target audience lives digitally or physically.
Instead of buying a broad ad, deploy a "raider" (an
ambassador or intern) to infiltrate that space with a high-value,
low-cost hook. Manufacture the crowd until it is real.

CH 10: THE SMOLDERING MAN | The Gas Can Pivot When
your "cinematic" plan fails, do not pause. Execute the backup
immediately with total confidence. The market rewards the

"whoosh" of the result, not the elegance of the intended process.

CH 11: THE BORDER CROSSING | The Dana Audit Identify the person in your office whose head contains all the vital tribal knowledge. If they weren't there tomorrow, would the system flatline? Begin flat-packing their logic into modular instructions immediately.

CH 12: THE NOMADIC PHALANX | The No-Silo Cross-Train Pick two departments that rarely speak (e.g., Sales and Accounting). Swap one team member from each for forty-eight hours. This eliminates the "hero bottleneck" and builds the role redundancy required for hyper-growth.

PART III: THE SUPERPOWER (HYPER-GROWTH TACTICS)

CH 13: THE HURRICANE | The "Irene" Pivot Look at your biggest recent failure, a canceled project or a lost client. Ask what new product exists in the eye of this storm. How can you turn a "No-Go" into a high-intensity offering for your most loyal believers?

CH 14: THE BEAST | The Complexity Moat Identify the "flat ground" parts of your business that are easily copied. How can you add verticality? Shift your focus toward the projects that make your competitors hesitate. Easy is a commodity; difficulty is a moat.

CH 15: THE TRIFECTA MACHINE | The Visual Void Audit Does the customer feel "finished" after one purchase? Design a three-part certification or a visual trophy system (like the Wedge Medal) to trigger the psychological need for symmetry. Sell the pieces of a soul, not just a ticket.

CH 16: THE GREEN MONSTER | The Sacred Space Identification Identify a venue, platform, or partnership that currently feels off-limits. Look for a residual gap in their schedule. Negotiate for the time when the "Cathedral" is dark and the owners are looking for supplementary revenue.

PART IV: THE LEGACY (UNBREAKABLE)

CH 17: THE GLOBAL SUPERPOWER | The Big Mac Test Identify the one "core value" of your product that must remain identical across every geography. If you stepped out of the room today and that standard would fail to hold up without your "magic touch," you haven't built a machine; you've built a job.

CH 18: THE VIRUS | The Box Drill Shrink your entire business logic into a single playbook that a stranger could operate. Shift your mindset from "Operator" to "Certifier." Move from a logistics-bound organization to a nimble model designed to scale quickly without infrastructure drag.

CH 19: THE OLYMPIC ASCENT | The Category King Rewrite Stop selling your features; start selling the result. Make your brand the synonym for the outcome. If you achieved your ten-year vision but your company name was erased from history, would you still do it?

CH 20: THE FRICTION ADVANTAGE | The Final Vector Technology and comfort are depreciating assets. The only value that appreciates over time is the ability to do hard things. Choose to be the whetstone rather than the pillow. Start one one-hundred-year project today that you will never see finished.

.

The Spartan Library: Fuel for the Forge

If *Becoming Spartan* is your map for navigating the friction of life and business, these works by Spartan Founder & CEO Joe De Sena are the fire that powers the engine. Explore the foundations of the movement:

- **Spartan Up!**
  - The *New York Times* Bestseller that started it all. A deep dive into the "Obstacle Immersion" philosophy and why we need to stop avoiding the hard things and start seeking them out.
- **Spartan Fit!**
  - The tactical guide to building a body that can handle the Navigator's Code. A 30-day training program designed to strip away the "Pillow" habits of modern life.
- **The Spartan Way**
  - A blueprint for resilience. Joe breaks down the 10 core principles—from commitment to delayed gratification—required to lead a life of purpose.
- **10 Rules for Resilience**
  - Mental toughness for a world in chaos. This is the manual for forging an unbreakable mind when the "Red Wedding" moments of life strike.
- **Extreme Balance**
  - A guide to achieving high-performance equilibrium. Learn how to navigate the demands of elite business, intense training, and family without sacrificing your core.
- **Ready for Anything**
  - A 52-week manual for grit. This year-long guide provides the weekly protocols necessary to stay in a state of constant readiness, no matter what the terrain looks like.
- **The Spartan One**

- o The foundation for the next generation. A story-driven guide designed to help children embrace the Spartan principles of courage and resilience early in life.
- **The Spartan Kids Workout**
  - o Tactical fitness for young Spartans. A practical program to help kids build physical strength and the mental toughness required to overcome any obstacle.

Navigator's Note: Each of these titles represents a pillar of the Spartan mindset. Read them to understand the "Why"; read *Becoming Spartan* to master the "How."

Scan QR Code for a Special Offer